A Life Worth Living

Li has not yet told all t]
1940s and 1950s Malay
her first volume, *The R*~~emoriant integram s Danguvin. In also again~~
us with further travel stories before detailing the decline and
eventual death of her husband of nearly 58 years. Her own
health concerns begin yet another journey.

Li's reflections lead her to realise that, with her roller coaster
ride of experiences, she has received much in this life. It has
been a life worth living!

A Life Worth Living

A second memoir by Zhang Li

ISBN 978-1-7636695-0-5

Dedication

To my sister Meng, quiet, unobtrusive, accepting her lot in life, expecting no rewards. Your concern and care helped to bring about a bolder, more challenging Li, who wrote the books on our unusual childhood.

Meng and Li in 1946

Contents

Forward 11

Re-introduction to Shanghai and the Zhang Family 13

Part 1 – The early years.. 17

Childhood Revisited 19

    A feast: Chinese steamboat dinner........................... 19

    A home performance 21

    Ah Foong, Empress of the Chamber Pots 22

    The chocolate thief 27

    Durians and the Zhang family 29

    Li learns who her parents are 31

    The ten dollar note with a hole in the centre 32

    Little Li, Afro princess... 33

    Yeh the songbird 34

    A near drowning... 36

    Meng, Li and the lightning bolt 38

    Body images 40

A Migrant's Pain, Zhang Yu's Funeral............................... 43

    The Buddhist ceremony: The monks at their prayers........... 46

    The migrants' contribution 50

    Growing up in a shophouse: late 1940s and early 1950s 51

    Serenade of the hawkers 53

    Li's neighbourhood: Growing up on Batu Road 55

    New clothes for Chinese New Year.......................... 58

    A love so pure: Li and Ah Chieh 59

The canings 65

The Journey.. 67

The Rise and Fall of the Zhang Family Fortunes 69

The Shanghai Dressmaking Co and Zhang Yu 70

One beautiful morning in May 1948............................ 72

Management issues 74

The money slowly starts to run out 75

The Story of Kit.. 79

Humour while in danger 79

Family matters 81

The Growing Years: 1950s 82

Part 2 – The middle years 89

Li the Young Lady 91

A Glimpse Into Early Married Life 94

Kit and me: A rented room 94

Yeh, Li and the Crown Prince of Brunei 96

The bad mother 98

1970 Travels.. 100

An encounter with Muhammad Ali 103

Grace, Jewellery and Mind Games........................... 105

The jade earrings.. 106

Know thyself: A last meeting with Grace 108

Part 3 – The later years 111

Happy Days of Travel 113

Cruising 113

Touring 114

Borobudur 115

Bali.. 116

South America.. 119

Argentina.. 119

Brazil.. 120

Peru 121

Cambodia 126

Vietnam.. 129

Turkey 130

My days of wine and roses.. 132

Hard Times: 2010s 135

Health problems.. 135

On safari 138

The fall and brain haemorrhage 141

2015: I am in trouble – an email brings bad tidings............ 147

The Mother: Self-reflection 151

Victoria Institution Global Reunion October 2015 153

Life Goes On: 2016 - 2017... 155

Old Age and Love 157

2018: A Sad Year 158

Tears.. 158

My last argument with Kit... 159

The disaster cruise: 2018 160

Return to Malaysia... 165

Move to Kuala Lumpur.. 170

Our last months in Malaysia 174

Trip to Malacca 176

The last Christmas 179

The Last Chinese New Year 182

Return to Sydney: The long journey home 184

Transfer to Concord Hospital 187

A journey ends 189

The funeral 191

Grief 194

Epilogue.. 195

Postscript 198

Glossary of selected characters 201

Papa, the Patriarch: Zhang Yu 201

MahMah, the Matriarch: Foong Ying.................. 201

Ah Chieh 202

Ah Heng Char 202

Zhang Jen, my father...................................... 203

Luk May, my mother....................................... 204

Songs of Bereavement 205

I remember 205

Where are you?.. 206

Here am I.. 207

Special Moments.. 208

A Journey's End 209

The Bench... 210

Sadness and Happiness 211

Together... 212

Ode to Ashes 213

A Song for the Aged 214

Acknowledgements.. 215

Editor's Note 216

Credits 219

Forward

It was 2023. I was pretty smug. My first memoir, *The Reluctant Migrant's Daughter*, was published and my second was finished. I thought I would leave this world soon and was prepared to go.

Writing *The Reluctant Migrant's Daughter* had been most painful, but it released the heaviness that sat on my chest for so many years. Yes, it was about the lonely unhappy child who had yearned for so much. But it was also a book about the people around her. The reluctant migrants who had left the land of their birth for a better future. These early migrants who hoped to return to their motherland with wealth and to die there.

The next generation of migrants had a very different philosophy. Kit and I were looking for a new home where our children could grow and develop. A country where they would enjoy political freedom and reach their full potential. That was our gift to our children. For ourselves, we wanted a country where we could grow old peacefully, a country we could love. A place where we could pass away peacefully and our ashes could be buried or cast into the river. This was the big difference. The new country was to be our home.

There was also a lesson to be learnt from my life.

In writing *The Reluctant Migrant's Daughter* and closely scrutinising my past, I learnt that I had been given much in life. From my lonely and unhappy childhood I developed independence and the ability to manage on my own.

From as far as back as I can remember I always had a fighting spirit. I cannot be subdued or do the bidding of others. I feel too strongly about what I perceive as injustice. I am what I am and do not need to apologise for it! But I also understand that in our moments of darkness there are lessons to be learnt and that we can gain strength. The strength we gain sustains and helps us to meet other challenges.

My guardian's taunts that I was of little value and would never amount to much were painful. So was my mother-in-law's observation that I brought no dowry, could not sing, draw or cook and played no musical instruments, so at least I should be obedient! Being told I had married above my station and my status as a wife was inferior to that of a mother gave me a crushing pain. But I did receive love and knew joy in my married life.

In all, I received much so that, by the age of 83, I developed a certain calmness and acceptance in the knowledge that life is unpredictable. Still, the diagnosis of cancer came as a shock! I had hoped for a pain-free exit, particularly after Kit's distressing departure, which had hit the family hard.

The chemotherapy was difficult to bear, followed by the operation. It was a dark time, yet surmountable. I go on to the next challenge, for my medical problems are not over.

So why a second memoir? There was so much that Li wanted to say in her first book but did not. It comes out here. Yes, more of the same. However, during this last year I have thought deeply about how some people think and felt the need to write again.

I am glad I do not hate. It is a negative emotion and can only hurt those who harbour it. I pity cousin Heng, described in this volume, who turned on me so viciously. He never knew the joy a family can bring. When I wrote my first book I had thought about Jen, my father, and MahMah, my guardian. Why were they so cold? I never wanted to hate them and I do not.

In this memoir I have also written about Kit's ill health and suffering. It is a warning of how cruel life can be. He seemed to have been given so much in life, yet he was dealt so many harsh blows. Nevertheless, he remained uncomplaining, gentle, optimistic, my Confucian gentleman.

I will be glad if my experiences encourage others to meet their challenges. It depends on the way we look at life. My memories are strong. There is much I can smile about. I conclude: it is a life worth living ...

ZL 13 May 2024

Re-introduction to Shanghai and the Zhang Family

Sometime in the 1890s two young brothers in Shanghai spoke of migration overseas, to the lands across the South China Sea, to South East Asia. By the end of the 19th century many from the southern provinces of China had migrated abroad, seeking to escape the poverty they endured at home. Few had migrated from the north. However, all Chinese migrants wanted a better life and hoped for wealth to take back to China.

So much had happened in China and so much more was to happen. Foreign aggression was spearheaded by the British with the Opium Wars that began in 1839. By the 1880s other western powers had pushed their way in. This was known as the cutting of the Chinese melon, and the Europeans and Americans all wanted a slice. The burning and sacking of the summer palace by the British and French troops in 1860, and again in the 1900 attack by the Eight-Nation Alliance, revealed all too well the rapacity of the foreigners and the weakness of the Chinese under the Manchus.

An inept, conservative government in decline, the Qing dynasty ruled China. These Manchu warrior "barbarians" had conquered China in 1644. The Manchus became sinicised in time, modelling themselves on the preceding Chinese dynasties.

The ethnic Chinese citizens insisted on calling themselves "Hans" to distinguish themselves from the Manchus, the invaders.

Unable or unwilling to change, Empress Cixi, an ambitious, xenophobic ruler, fell victim to the western powers. She was more successful in Court intrigues and manipulation than in ruling the nation. The Boxer Uprising of 1900 was a weak attempt to evict the foreigners. At a most critical time China failed to meet the challenges from the West and the Qing Dynasty fell in 1911.

The brothers Zhang lived through these turbulent times. The younger brother was my grandfather, so this Chinese history is not to me something dead, but personal.

But back to the Shanghai of the 1920s, to the environment and the thinking of that time.

The British and French were well-established in the Shanghai International Settlement. The others had followed: Germans, Italians, Belgians and Austrians. Neighbouring Russia was always in the background. The influx of Russian Jews during and after the fall of Tsarist Russia also assisted in the development of Shanghai. They expanded the Jewish community which followed the trading Iraqi-born British Sassoon family into China some decades earlier.

Shanghai had grown into a successful commercial and banking centre, not least on the back of the opium trade. Did this contribute to the thinking of the Zhang brothers and to Zhang Yu's desire to take Shanghai's world of fashion to Malaya? The Zhangs were a minority amongst the largely peasant Chinese population – it was not physical labour they were offering, but business acumen.

In 1929 their plans came to fruition, for elder brother Zhang made his reconnaissance journey to Kuala Lumpur. By then a new person had joined the family, Zhang Yu, who was a member of the group that travelled to Kuala Lumpur.

Zhang Yu had the same surname but was not related. He was employed by my granduncle, Elder brother Zhang, and his initiative, intelligence and capacity for hard work did not go unnoticed. He proved himself to be the best worker in the Zhang family fashion business, and shared Elder brother Zhang's vision of a business overseas. They had much in common. My granduncle had only one child, his daughter Foong Ying. She married Zhang Yu with her father's blessing.

Zhang Yu was indeed the son my granduncle wanted. Granduncle was too old to make a new life for himself overseas, but Zhang Yu was the person to do it.

My grandfather also felt he was too old to start a new life overseas. His young son Jen, my father, would be sent to join the family business in a few years' time. Grandfather also had three daughters. He would stay in Shanghai with them.

In 1932, Jen left Shanghai with his new bride Luk May. He had been perfectly happy with his life in Shanghai, but it was his father's wish that he go, and he would never disobey his father. His marriage had been arranged and Luk May was such a lovely person. Father knows best!

And so Jen and Luk May settled in Kuala Lumpur. They had seven children there, plus Hoong, the youngest, who was born in Shanghai in 1948.

Li's family

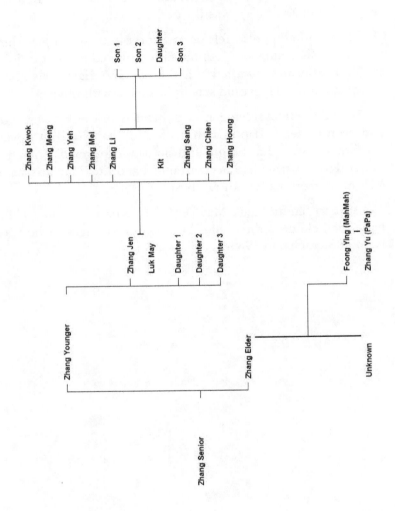

Part 1 – The early years

Childhood Revisited

Sister Meng and I are now in our eighties, nearing the end of our journey in this earthly life. We often return to our childhood days. Perhaps this happens to all old people. Before I fall asleep, the images that flash past are the figures of my siblings and me as children …

I recall the six-year-old Li, laughing and giggling as she crunched on a piece of green apple. (They were from Thailand, just across the northern border, plentiful and cheap.) Only twenty minutes before the scene had been so different. Li had been caned. She stood in the corner with big drops of tears running down her cheeks. It was her first year of caning.

Ah Chieh had found her and given her a big piece of apple, for she knew little Li needed consolation.

In no time Li was telling Ah Chieh that the neighbour's cat was fat and had a big belly. She was told that the cat had kittens in her belly. Li had touched the belly and recoiled when she felt a movement. It was such a delightful experience that she had burst out in giggles, as she did while relating the incident. Li was resilient, with so much capacity for laughter and happiness. Young children forgive so readily.

In my reverie, the monsoon rains have started with the heavy downpours, lightning and thunder. Li is frightened and runs off to look for sister Meng. Meng puts a protective arm around a tearful Li, telling her it would pass in a moment. It was only a short thunderstorm.

Ahhh … childhood!!

A feast: Chinese steamboat dinner

The excitement of Little Li's first Chinese steamboat dinner is memorable. Li, aged five, sits next to Ah Chieh and eats everything placed in her bowl, for every morsel is delicious. She is too small to stand and participate in the cooking.

Meng sits next to PaPa, while Kwok is next to MahMah. Yeh sits next to Kwok.

On the large round dining table is an array of meats: plates of raw chicken, beef, pork and the pork entrails, liver and kidneys that the Chinese love. There are prawns and home-made fish balls as well. Steamboat dinners are also about vegetables: lettuce, spinach, water convolvulus and, on the largest plate, the cabbage that the Shanghainese love most of all, wong buk. Business is good, so the Zhangs can afford to eat well.

There is a shout from the cook emerging from the kitchen: 'Boiling water coming!'

With a towel in each hand, the cook carries out a large steamboat and places it on a wooden board in the middle of the table. The bottom of the boat has a cavity filled with small live pieces of charcoal to keep the soup boiling. The soup is made from hours of boiling pork and chicken bones together and is so delicious that everyone has more than one bowl. The boat was brought from Shanghai, as was the red Chinese porcelain crockery. This is a favourite meal of the Shanghainese and a "must have" during the cold Shanghai winters.

To a loud cheer, Zhang Yu lifts the lid of the steamboat. The adults rise and empty the plates of food into the boiling soup. The mood is one of joy and merriment. The meat and vegetables do not take long to cook and the looks of anticipation turn to satisfaction as the diners bite into the tasty morsels. The food disappears quickly from the steamboat with the help of slotted metal serving spoons, while a long ladle scoops out the soup. Fresh soup from the kitchen tops up the depleting volume in the boat. Cups of Chinese wine for the adults also add to the gaiety.

Ah Chieh helps to feed Li. The child is getting to be expert in managing the porcelain spoon, which enters her little mouth without difficulty. She is quick to empty the food from her bowl. Li loves good food.

PaPa is most tactful as he ensures that MahMah's bowl is always full, only then helping Ah Chieh. MahMah transfers food from her bowl to Kwok's. PaPa also sees to it that Meng is fed, while Ah Chieh helps with Yeh and Li. Ah Chieh also has a soft spot for Yeh. Li can see how happy everyone is.

In later years, when the Zhang children are tall and old enough to place food into the boat, there are accusations of food theft. Li often accuses Yeh of stealing her food. Where did the two prawns and fish balls disappear to? Yeh is a fast eater and not that innocent! While Li searches for her fish balls in the steamboat, Yeh wears a grin that spreads from ear to ear!

A home performance

Clap, clap, clap! Little Li brings her chubby hands together as she always does when she is happy. Her round face is lit up with joy. She is given a front seat as Ah Chieh performs in front of the Zhang family. The servants and housemaids are allowed to watch. It is an impromptu performance.

Ah Chieh starts by juggling five round objects, three oranges and two apples.

Up they go in the air, higher and higher. Ah Chieh catches them expertly. She goes on to the next scene, throwing a dessert-sized plate into the air and catching it with a stick. Soon there are four plates spinning on four sticks in each of Ah Chieh's hands. Oh how they spin! Li is mesmerised. In her heart, little Li silently calls out 'Ah Chieh I love you, you are soooo clever.' Li has been taught not to let out her emotions!

In the audience is MahMah, with Kwok seated beside her. She is enjoying the performance. PaPa wears a smile, as he enjoys watching Ah Chieh too. The other Zhang children are seated around the room.

Before the last scene starts Ah Chieh explains the basic emotions the actor must master if he or she hopes to perform in the Peking Opera. Ah Chieh pulls up a seat in front of the audience. She begins by showing the emotion Joy. She shows a happy, smiling face. With a hand movement as if she is wiping her face, the laughing face turns to one of anger. Ah Chieh's face is contorted and her eyes fired up. She shows great rage. She wipes her face again and this time there is coyness and beguiling eyes. It is the face of a young maiden looking up at her lover. Her hand moves across the face again to wipe off the emotion and to present a new one. This time Ah Chieh shows grief and sadness as she pretends to cry. Little Li bursts into sobs. Sister Meng rushes over to quieten Li, telling her it is pretence, not real. Ah Chieh continues a while more. Soon the show is over and everyone gets up. Everyone is happy. It has been a good day, a good dinner, followed by Ah Chieh's performance. MahMah smiles occasionally as she goes off to bed. She does enjoy shows.

Fast forward to 1993 in Sydney, Australia. Ah Chieh does the juggling act with the plates to entertain the guests at Li's home dinner party. Ah Chieh has lost neither her performing skills nor her cooking skills, for she has added her excellent dumplings to Li's curry dishes. All these she had learnt while training for so many years to be a Peking Opera performer.

Ah Foong, Empress of the Chamber Pots

Little Li is five and learning to discriminate between 'nice' and 'not nice' people. She learns from Ah Heng's sharp tongue and sarcasm. Ah Heng Char is the most important maid in the Zhang household. She has looked after Weng, the eldest son of Zhang Yu and Ah Chieh. The child is doted upon by MahMah, who runs the domestic household. Ah Heng is MahMah's confidante. All the housemaids are frightened of Ah Heng, and so is little Li. Ah Heng's pet nickname for Li is 'little worm', but Li does not resent her.

Ah Heng tells of a powerful empress in China, Empress Cixi, who ruled a vast empire. Although the Empress had passed away there were still many princes and princesses. Li remembers all Ah Heng's stories.

Little Li is hovering around when Ah Foong's mother brings her to work as a maid at the shophouse. Ah Foong is barely fifteen, but is already physically developed. Li notices that the workers at the dry cleaning shop always look whenever she passes, but could see that Ah Foong is not interested. She is there to earn a salary for her mother. Her goal is to become a seamstress and ultimately to own her own little dressmaking shop.

Ah Foong annoys Li, for she knocks Li's head with the comb each morning when doing her plaits. Besides looking after Li, Ah Foong has other duties, the most important of which is cleaning the chamber pots.

'Yes, I shall name Ah Foong "Empress of the Chamber Pots" because she is mean to me', Li says to herself.

At that time we have running water in town, but no modern sanitation. MahMah, who had grown up in a single storey house in China, never goes down to the toilets behind the shops to empty her bowels like everyone else, even the children.

'Beat her, beat her, she is the only one you can smack in this household', meaning Li, Ah Foong tells a new housemaid who has just started work. 'Ah Chieh checks on her, but you can always get away with it by saying she is naughty and stubborn and that she is a cry-baby.

'The power in this house lies with the senior wife, Foong Ying. Even her husband is afraid of her. Ah Chieh is only a junior wife and has no authority. Stay away from the other children, especially Kwok. Meng is quite harmless and so is Yeh.

'Foong Ying dotes on little Weng, child of Zhang Yu and Ah Chieh. She is still fond of Kwok and spoils him, so do not offend him.

'But Li, she is a strange one. She locks her eyes on you. Her eyes probe into you as if she can read your thoughts. For that reason I do not like her', says Ah Foong.

The new maid never finds out for herself. Her father turns up to take her home in less than a week. His stall is doing good business and his daughter no longer needs to work as a housemaid!

Besides good food, Ah Foong gets outings as one of the perks of her job. Entertainment in the late 1940s in Kuala Lumpur includes what are known as the Amusement Parks. The bigger one is Bukit Bintang Park, named after the road. The smaller one is Lucky World, which is not far from Batu Road. Li visits it when she goes on her walkabouts a few years later.

Within BB Park, as the locals call it, is a large Cantonese Opera Theatre, very popular with opera buffs. There is a joget dance stage, where you can do Malay dancing with young Malay girls if you buy a ticket. Li enjoys listening to the Malay dance music and always lingers next to the stage. There are also pinball stalls.

BB Dance Hall and main entrance to the BB Park in 1953

The most posh and classy place is the BB Cabaret. Here you can do western dancing. There is a western band, a singer and pretty young Chinese girls with whom you can dance if you buy drinks. This is currently the place to find the rich bachelors, largely from rich Chinese families.

(In Form 3, my dear classmate and friend confided in me that her mother was a dancer there. She fell for the band leader and she, the daughter, was the result!

Lucky World c. 1953

For some years at Lucky World there is a talented Chinese performing troupe. Two sisters who can sing and dance are popular. The troupe produces dances, comedy sketches and scenes from the Peking Opera. All you pay for is coffee. If you stay you are expected to buy a second coffee, as well as order a plate of peanuts. The latest Mandarin songs are sung, including patriotic Chinese songs. Li hears a rumour that communist agents can be found relaxing at the show while government agents spy on them as they mingle in the audience. The British Government later banned the communist party in Malaya.

Ah Chieh has given Li an interest in Chinese songs and she visits the Lucky World many times on her later walkabouts.

Back to Ah Foong. If the children are given money for supper, the housemaids are also given money to enjoy supper. This is often fried noodles in dark sauce or wantons and barbecue pork in soup. The housemaids enjoy the rickshaw rides and the bright lights, which don't exist in the villages.

Ah Foong is from a village and is used to cold water. Ah Heng complains about her 15 minute showers. Ah Foong also has a foot fetish, scrubbing her toe nails with a toothbrush so they are always pink and clean!

There are many housemaids at the Zhang residence, but they come and go. In most cases, Li only remembers that she is cleaned and fed by them. Ah Foong stays the longest.

When Ah Foong came Ah Chieh had started having her own children and MahMah had begun to regard Li and Yeh as superfluous and irrelevant. Ah Foong is aware of this and is quite hard on Li. Her constant labelling of Li as smelly and dirty ensures that the child has no attachment to her. Decades later, Sister Meng said Ah Foong was hard working and not malicious.

Li wants to be cleaned the same way as MahMah, who never touches cold water. MahMah has a big basin of warm water brought to her as she sits on a stool and sponges herself with a little towel. Lastly, she soaks her feet as more hot water is added. That was how it was done in her days in Shanghai and so she continues the habit. Ah Chieh adapts and bathes in cold water, emptying buckets of cold water over herself. This is the tropics and this makes her feel clean and refreshed.

Ah Foong is no sentimentalist. She does what is asked of her, but tolerates no nonsense from Li. One day Li almost collides into Ah Foong, who is carrying two chamber pots and can't wait to get rid of them. They have wooden covers but still they smell. Ah Foong does not like Li watching her. She calls out to Li: 'One day when I leave this job you will be the one to take over, then you will have to wash the chamber pots.' Li quickly runs off in fear. She does not want to be Empress of the Chamber Pots!

Ah Foong did leave the housemaid's job and trained as a seamstress under Ching. She achieved her ambition of running a little dressmaking shop in Singapore.

The chocolate thief

'Beat Li, beat Li, smack her. She has done something bad. She stole sister Meng's chocolates.' Meng smacks her. Li does not run away but stands still with guilt written all over her face.

That morning when Meng sees her, Li runs away from, instead of to, Meng with her usual chatter. Meng knows instinctively that something is up. She runs after Li and catches her. Meng sees a faint trace of chocolate on Li's lips.

Meng had hidden two pieces of chocolate the day before, after coming home from Hilda's house. Hilda always had chocolates for the children. She and Kwok had gone there to play. She had wrapped the chocolates in a napkin and carefully put them in a drawer to hide them from Kwok, who would have gobbled them up if he got his hands on them. She had escaped Kwok only to fall foul of Li!

Kwok, Yeh and Meng in front of Hilda's mansion c. 1940

Yeh, Hilda and Meng c. 1943

Meng runs to the drawer only to find that the white napkin with its treasure is gone. She flies to Li's bed, knowing Li keeps her precious things under her pillow. She whips up Li's smelly pillow to see two colourful chocolate wrappers. Li cannot resist pretty items. Here is the incriminating evidence. Li is definitely guilty. She has not run away, nor has she cried, but allows herself to be smacked. Li is normally an honest child, but this time she has stolen Meng's chocolates. She loves food, particularly sweet things.

The day before Li had been sitting in the far corner of the sitting room examining her fingers. She thought she had the nicest looking fingers. They were chubby, and nobody had chubby fingers like hers. Then she heard a sound. It was Meng cautiously moving across towards the cupboard in her bedroom. The bedroom door was wide open and Meng did not see her. As usual, no one noticed Li. Meng popped something into the drawer and ran off.

Li waited a while, then moved to the drawer, opened it and found the napkin covering the two beautifully foil-wrapped chocolates. Li's eyes glowed. Of course she recognised them. She had been at Hilda's a month ago and was given one. They were the yummiest chocolates in the whole world! That night Li ate one of them. The next morning after breakfast, greedy five year old Li ate the other. 'Sorry Meng, I had to have it.'

Meng is often kind to Li, giving her sweets. She also allows Li to look at her picture books. Sometimes Meng gives her a biscuit. Li enjoys it, even if it is half chewed, with Meng's teeth marks on it. Li loves food.

Durians and the Zhang family

Durian is a tropical fruit, the King of Fruits. It is also known as the fruit of kings, as the Malay sultans loved it. Some who cannot resist durian describe its taste as out of this world. The flesh of the fruit just melts in your mouth, no biting or chewing required. Yet it is avoided and detested by others. Why? The large fruit emits a strong smell that many find disgusting, calling it the stinky fruit or saying it tastes like eating custard in the toilet. How can a fruit evoke such diametrically opposed reactions?

What about the Zhang family? The reaction to durian was diverse. MahMah tolerated it. She was used to foods with strong smells. The smelly fermented bean curd, tow foo, was a favourite of hers. So too a certain smelly bean. She did not eat durian herself, probably because it was foreign, but she did not mind others eating it. PaPa tried it but it left him lukewarm. However, Ah Chieh acquired a taste for durian, just as she did to the cold showers that all locals enjoyed. PaPa would buy it for her and as a treat for the Zhang children, who loved it.

'Ha ha, look at Li, she is eating three pieces at a time', laughed Ah Chieh. 'She has one in her mouth, one in her chubby hand, and her eyes are focussed on the fruit in the chamber right in front of her.' The delicious flesh came wrapped around large seeds in four or five chambers in each durian.

The five year old was savouring the succulent fruit, oblivious to the chatter around. She was concentrating, while the others, Kwok, Meng and Yeh, were eating at a faster pace.

Half an hour later there was an agonised roar. It came from Jen. One of the children had used Jen's towel to wipe their hand, leaving behind the smell! Jen hated the odour of durians, but could not protest as it was Zhang Yu who bought them. Jen accepted all Yu's decisions. He respected and adored Yu. Later in his own home Jen never allowed durian eating. Although Luk May loved the fruit she could only eat it elsewhere. She had to scrub her hands and ensure there was no residual smell on her before going home.

Jen never understood why others could not stick to watermelon, which could be so sweet. Watermelon was common in Shanghai during summer and even more so in Malaya, where it was available the whole year round. Why did members of the Zhang family go seeking the foul smelling durian?

Li learns who her parents are

It is late 1945 and Li has gone looking for Ah Chieh, for she has bumped her knee hard against the dining table and it is hurting. Instead, she walks into a cranky looking MahMah, the last person she wants to see. From Meng she has learnt to run away and hide from MahMah, of whom sister Meng is terrified. Meng is not subjected to caning, but the tongue lashings often leave her in tears. The caning has not started yet for Li, but she can get a rap on the head from MahMah's knuckles!

MahMah is in a foul mood, probably from a disagreement with Zhang Yu. She looks at the child and asks 'Are you looking for Ah Chieh? She is busy with her own second child and has no time for you. Do you not know she is not your mother?'

Li is confused. She does not quite know what the words "father" and "mother" mean, but there is an older housemaid at this time who has been kind. Li seeks her out. She learns that these are terms for one's parents. She learns, too, that her biological parents are the people all the Zhang children called Ah Sook and Ah Sum, auntie and uncle. The housemaid thought this may be customary among the Shanghainese, as Zhang Yu was the patriarch and Foong Ying the matriarch, thus PaPa and MahMah. The kindly housemaid also tries to explain that only biological parents are obliged to look after children and that Li cannot expect care from others.

Li is still confused but she slowly starts to learn. Once Li had wanted to run to Zhang Yu and hug his legs, but MahMah shooed her off. He was not her father and she had no right to even hug him. She had no right to Ah Chieh either. Did the child have a right to love anyone?

31

The ten dollar note with a hole in the centre

Little Li is growing fast. She is going to turn seven soon. Two weeks before she had followed Meng and Yeh to the candy shop more than a block away. She now knows the way there. She searches out Ah Chieh.

Highly elated, she describes to Ah Chieh the array of goods the shop sells. Half the front of the shop is covered by a display of candies. There are ginger pieces in large glass jars – salted, pickled, sweetened, spicy. There is a whole range of plums – sweet, sour, brown and black, small, medium or large in size, with or without seeds. Sister Meng paid five cents and got eight plums. Li and Yeh were given one each. Li even got to meet fourteen year old Ah Huai, the shopkeeper and owner's eldest son. He served them and was so nice. On and on she prattles. With a wave of her hand and a note of finality, she tells Ah Chieh she is perfectly able to walk there by herself.

Two weeks later Ah Chieh and little Li are alone in the sitting room. Ah Chieh has something to say. 'I dropped some money a few days ago.' No response from Li. Li is examining her toes. 'Ouch, ouch', she touches her big toes with their recently cut nails. 'They are painful', she moans. 'Why did the housemaid have to cut so deep?'

Ah Chieh tries again. 'I wonder if torn money gets accepted in shops. What if a note had a hole in the centre. Surely a shopkeeper will not accept it!'

This time Li jumps up and shouts. 'Yes they will, even a ten dollar note with a hole in the middle. Just you wait. I am going to get something from under my pillow.' Li runs off with a smile. She is cleverer than Ah Chieh. She knows something Ah Chieh does not!

Li runs back carrying a little package, a small handkerchief with something wrapped in the middle. Li unties the knots of the handkerchief. Out come the dollar notes and coins. Nine dollars and eighty five cents. Li had splurged a whole fifteen cents on sweet and sour plums. The shopkeeper had been honest although he had stared at Li. He must have been puzzled about how the child had got so much money.

A few days ago Li had found the torn note at the corner of the room. Ah Chieh smiled. So it was Li who found the note, not one of the housemaids.

Yes, nothing escaped Li's sharp eyes. She had seen a reddish piece of paper in the corner of the room and had gone to investigate. To her amazement, she unfolded a ten dollar note! Li is not a stranger to money. She has seen notes in the shop till. She has seen purchases take place. As her eyes sparkled and danced Li's immediate thought was not to question where the money had come from, but that it was going to buy her lots and lots of yummy candies!

Little Li, Afro princess

Ha ha ha, hee hee hee … everyone burst out laughing as little Li entered the room, even Ah Chieh. There stood the most miserable looking eight year old. Small, slightly tanned, scrawny and with tears in her eyes. Her hair had been burnt by her first perm. It was curly, rather woolly-looking and standing upright, probably the first Afro style in Malaya. After the perm Li had seen herself in the mirror and hid in her room. But she emerged at lunchtime.

Earlier that morning Ah Foong, the housemaid, had knocked her head again with the hardwood brown comb and Li was crying again. The disturbance had reached MahMah, who reacted immediately. MahMah instructed Ah Foong to take Li downstairs to have her hair permed and put an end to the crying. A new hairdressing salon had been established with

Lao San, Ah Chieh's sister, in charge. Zhang Yu had given permission for the vacant second floor to be used and provided the capital. Lao San seemed to be talented at hairdressing and enjoyed it. It made Ah Chieh most happy.

There was a new perming machine and a whole lot of wires and clips. Li found the process painful as the perming lotion was applied to her hair, which was then pulled tight, rolled up and connected to the clips. Lao San had checked and declared they needed another minute to make sure that Li's straight hair became curly. The next time the assistant looked, the hair was burnt. They did not realise that Li had a curly hair base inherited from father Jen. Lao San told Li that she would give her a trim in a fortnight and everything would be normal again.

(In 1982 Li had allowed an Australian hairdresser to give her a soft perm and the same thing happened, although it was not as bad. Li made the hairdresser "wash out" the perm and never had her hair permed again.)

Good thing it was school holidays. At least Li would not have to face her classmates. At this stage Li thought of herself as the ugliest girl in the world. She already looked like a little rat with a scrawny face and two large front teeth. She did not need woolly hair as well. Lao San did give her that trim. Li now had a short crop with less of the wooliness.

Li was back to her lively self again. She was resilient.

Yeh the songbird

Writing this memoir triggered something about Yeh that I had forgotten. Yeh was the only one in the family who could sing. I remember his voice, which was sweet and clear. Those years were when he was six to twelve years of age, after which he stopped singing.

In 1946 Yeh's favourite song was the one he learnt from his nearby new school, the Batu Road School, an English establishment. 'BRS, BRS, hallelujah....' He was happy there and often sang the song. Each morning he cheerfully walked off to school. His new white canvas rubber-soled shoes, joined by the shoelaces, hung round his neck as he took off, bare footed. The shoes were so precious to him he would not put them on until just before the school gates, where the teachers would check that he wore them.

Yeh also often sang after he was caned. I felt this was to relieve himself after the sad moments.

As a child Yeh was bullied by brother Kwok. Seniority mattered in Chinese families. The elder brother was told he was more important and that he was owed obedience from the younger siblings, so bullying was not uncommon in Chinese families.

Yeh had no one to turn to. Ah Chieh liked him. She found his sensitive face appealing, but she did not have much time to spare. I took up some of that time before she had her children. Ah Chieh was walking on coals and had to watch where she stepped. MahMah was difficult to understand and Ah Chieh could not afford to offend her. She had two sisters and a mother to worry about.

Brother Yeh, aged X and Y

Yeh was the gentlest person in the world, I felt when recollecting our childhood. He stood still and silent when he was caned, no protest, no crying. In his last year of caning he was tall and strong enough to push over MahMah. I remember him saying that, but he never touched her. He must have practised great control. I do not know whether he realised that our father would have thrashed him half to death if he ever resisted her!

I remember so well my one and only fight with Yeh, because he refused to fight. He had accidentally torn my only comic book. I was hell-bent on revenge, even though I was a small eight year old. I started by pummelling him. He tried to escape but I clung to the belt of his shorts and was dragged into the sitting room. He gave me a shove. I lost balance and ended up falling right in front of the earth god's altar, hitting my head on the wooden floor.

Freed of me, he ran downstairs and out of the shop.

Ah Heng, the housekeeper, heard the noise and came out of the kitchen to see the scene unfold. Coincidentally, I fell ill and had a slight temperature for the next two days. I was never a physically strong child, unlike sister Mei. (I was the runt in the family.) Ah Heng told the others that the earth god had punished me for creating a scene at his altar instead of showing respect and kowtowing. She also told MahMah that Yeh deserved two extra strokes of the cane for offending the earth god!

A near drowning

It must have been early 1948 when Yeh and Li had their longest stay with their parents, lasting a few weeks, before Jen and Luk May returned to China for almost a year. Every now and then the temperamental and unpredictable MahMah felt that these two children needed to be sent back to their parents.

So Yeh and Li went to stay at the large wooden house on stilts in a compound in Yap Kwan Seng Road. The rent was cheap and it was also available for sale cheaply. But the Zhang family did not believe in investing locally. All wealth must be saved and taken back to Shanghai, not frittered away in Malaya.

36

The large compound had many trees, including some five guava trees. I remember that Mei, who was nine at the time, had become very good at climbing. She would stay on her favourite guava tree for ages, consuming the fruits with the pink centres, for they were the sweetest of the various fruits growing in the compound.

It was a fine day when Li convinced Yeh to take her to one of the mining ponds not too far from the house. These were places where labourers had dug for alluvial tin. They had been lucrative for a few years, but abandoned as the tin became scarce. Slowly, the mined areas, which could be extensive, had filled with water. The land was treacherous, uneven with sudden drops, but the local youths would go to swim there.

Brother Yeh was persuaded, but he had been instructed to keep an eye on Sang, who was one and a half years younger than Li. Yeh decided to bring Sang along. So the three children, aged eleven, eight and six, made their way to the nearby mining pond.

The moment Li spotted the pond she clapped her hands, a habit since she was three. The children quickened their steps and were soon at the water's edge. Li was keen to get in, and so was Sang, but Yeh was cautious. With Sang on one side of Yeh and Li on the other, the children waded in. Suddenly Sang disappeared. Only some of his thick hair showed above water. Yeh lunged and grabbed the hair. He shouted to Li to hold on to the belt of his shorts as he hauled Sang out of the water. As Yeh pulled, Sang's head appeared, followed by an outstretched arm, which a quick-thinking Yeh grabbed. The two older children managed to drag Sang out of the water. Sang coughed but managed to tell us that his feet had slipped. Yeh's quick actions meant that Sang had swallowed little water. They made their way home.

Three wet children were met by an anxious mother. Father Jen had gone on his motorbike to the shop for work. Yeh told Luk May that they had been playing at the water's edge. But she knew it must have been more than that, because Sang was totally soaked. She grabbed her soft slipper and proceeded to whack Li, who was standing closest to her. The soft Shanghainese slipper did not hurt like the cane. But Li jumped around and pretended to be in pain. She even managed to grin and wink at Yeh while Luk May was bent over, seriously concentrating on smacking Li's legs. Yeh was, of course, vigorously smacked with the slipper. As usual he stood still and received his punishment without protest. Li was the irrepressible child, while Yeh was the serious and responsible one. Yeh never let out that Li was behind the visit to the pond. Neither did the parents know that, but for Yeh, their favourite son Sang would have drowned.

A note on the soft Shanghainese slipper. These were slippers Luk May wore most of her life. They were of lightweight padded cotton. The covering of the slipper was usually embroidered with flowers, but sometimes with birds, or, now and again, a pair of mandarin ducks. Luk May's younger sister, our seventh aunt who lived in Hong Kong, sent them at six monthly intervals. Luk May would distribute them to her daughters and we all wore them growing up, even after marriage. I received my two pairs every year. Then, in the early 1970s, the government reclassified them as luxury goods. The tax cost more than the purchase price, so Luk May rejected the dozen pairs, which were returned to her sister in Hong Kong. She told her not to send anymore. The frugal Luk May had some pairs saved up. I brought my last pair with me to Australia. I liked them so much I wore them to shreds.

Meng, Li and the lightning bolt

It is the rainy season. The skies have been dark all morning, but by noon are streaked with flashes of lighting. Li is about eight years of age, small and skinny, fearfully cowering in the corner of the Zhang children's top floor sitting room. Meng is composed, seated and bent over a story book, untroubled. There is no mother to run to. Their mother is in another country, Li thinks. Anyway, she hardly knows her mother, seeing little of her.

The thunder gets louder. It is a particularly fierce equatorial storm. Li shudders each time the lighting flashes. Meng tells her that these storms last only an hour or so, but Li wants it to 'please go away.' Suddenly rings the loudest thunderclap Li had ever heard, followed by a short silence and the sound of falling brickwork and dust in the far corner of the room. The shophouse has been hit by lighting!

Li scampers to Meng, throwing her arms out in fear. The older, more practical Meng breaks free, yelling for Li to follow her to the opposite corner of the room in case more brickwork falls or the roof collapses!

But the storm has ended. There is no visible damage to the exterior of the shop. The aftermath is just a single small pile of debris in the top floor living quarters and a frightened child!

Three hours later everything is back to normal. Meng is reading her book and Li is seated on the wooden floor playing with her paper cuttings. A weak sun has appeared outside, although the roads are still wet and the drains full of water.

The two girls looked up as a person appears at the top of the stairs.

A middle aged plumpish woman, a stranger, has found her way into the Zhang living quarters. She has heard about the lighting strike and wants two pieces of the brickwork. Meng points to the debris, which has not been cleared. The woman smiles at the girls, telling them she is going to boil some of the broken bricks with herbs. Superstition has it that this is a cure for all ailments, as well as a preventive. The woman hurries away with her prizes.

Meng returns to her book. Li keeps gazing at the top of the staircase where the woman had stood. What an odd person!

Body images

'You shameless slut. You were seen naked in the neighbour's backyard, which is also their work area. You had not a stitch on, cavorting in the water tank, which is used for soaking pieces of plank for making furniture.

'Chinese females do not display their bodies. Only the husband may look at it. Do you deny you were naked?

'Answer me!' MahMah glares at Li.

'No, I do not deny it!'

MahMah continues 'Two years ago I told you that you were a good for nothing, that prostitution was your only route forwards! Am I ever wrong? Sixteen generations ago your ancestors committed a serious wrong and that brought about your birth. Must I be disturbed to discipline you? Do you need a caning session all to yourself?'

That night little eight year old Li examines her body. There are welts on her legs and her bottom is painful, for she has been caned there as well. She whispers to herself. 'I do not like my body. I do not mind my legs for they carry me about. My bottom is not too bad as it takes the cane well. My chest is absolutely flat, unlike Ah Chieh's. I do not like breasts, they get in the way! But I have been good to my body, I give it lots of snacks and yummy candy.'

That morning Li had gone to the shophouse where her friend and neighbour, Dee, lived with her family. Her father had a double shop as they need the space to display furniture. Dee told Li that the water tank out the back had been drained and refilled so the water was clean and we could play there. There we were at the side of the water tank. Dee took off her top, keeping her long pants on. Li took off her dress, keeping on her panties. She looked around. There was not a soul in sight so she took off her panties as well. Why? Promiscuous? No. If she went home with wet clothes, Ah Foong, the housemaid who sort of looked after her, would tell on her and Li would be caned. Of late Ah Foong seemed to delight in snitching on Li. The thought came to her mind: 'Keep the clothes dry so I do not get into trouble.'

By the time Li got home news of her misadventure had reached brother Yeh. Yeh was highly respected by the back lane boys, although he had started to withdraw-from their company. One of the boys had run over to our house to tell Yeh that their new leader, Ah Dere, was having a swim with Yeh's sister and that his sister had no clothes on! Yeh was very angry. He felt humiliated and ticked off Li. Li protested that when the boys appeared they had grabbed their clothes and ran off. She could only hang her head in shame.

How did a small innocent incident get blown out of proportion? It was an eight year old and a seven year old playing with water. They wanted a bit of fun. (Dee later told Li she was not punished, as her mother felt she did no wrong.)

At that age Li had little idea of her body. Nobody spoke about the body, its functions, least of all procreation. Talk of sex was taboo. All her mother ever said to Li about growing up was when she started menstruating at thirteen and Luk May handed Li a belt for menstrual pads.

'The movable part is in front, the fixed part at the back.' That was the sum total of Li's sex education.

At the age of eight Li learnt that breasts grow as a female grows. MahMah was flat chested, as was Ah Heng the housekeeper. Little Li wanted to be flat chested like them!

However, at the age of 18 Li was glad not to be flat chested, but was also happy she did not have a big chest. She wanted a neat, trim shape. Surrounded as she was by slim figures, full busted women appeared vulgar and un-Chinese!

Li aged 18

A Migrant's Pain, Zhang Yu's Funeral

Little Li was nine years old. It was the morning after Zhang Yu's body was brought back to the shophouse from the hospital. He had passed away. They could not save him. Zhang Yu had suddenly collapsed and thrown up blood, coughing out more blood and falling over. He had been rushed to the General Hospital, the biggest and the best in Kuala Lumpur.

He was returned to the shop in the late afternoon. His wives, MahMah and Ah Chieh decided to dress him in his long Chinese gown. They selected his favourite, the one he wore to special Chinese functions. He was placed on a wooden platform with a big ice bath underneath to slow down the decay. The platform was placed towards the back of the shop, which was emptied of all the display cupboards and items. Even the work area was cleared of sewing machines. To little Li the shop was now a vast cavernous area with only Zhang Yu. He was covered with a silk Chinese blanket, the coffin yet to arrive. Zhang Yu lay in peace in his beloved dressmaking shop. He was in Nangyang and had fulfilled his dream. He had brought fashion to Malaya.

Many mourners arrived by mid-morning on the next day.

A tall man dressed in a long Chinese gown walked towards Zhang Yu's body. He was the father of my friend Dee. His face was wet, for he had been crying. His best friend had suddenly died. He raised his hands, clasped in the Chinese salute. In a voice stricken with grief he called out Zhang Yu's name.

'My brother, I offer you three salutes to show what kind of man you were. Di yi zhi gong, my first salute (as he bowed in the direction of the body), is for what you were to me. We are fellow migrants. You came a bit earlier than me. You thought I did not know, you handed funds to my wife to buy food, for

43

I was struggling to earn a living. You helped me in my hour of need. Dear fellow Shanghainese, you treated me like a brother.

'My second salute, Di erh zi goong, is for the help you rendered to our fellow Shanghainese migrants. You helped start the association and were the president. Many fellow Shanghainese arrived in this new country with virtually the clothes they were wearing. You helped, through the association, to feed and clothe them. I thank you on their behalf.

'My third salute, Di san zhi goong, is to you as a family head. You worked day and night to feed the Zhang family. Your own children are only five, three and one. I grieve for them.

'May the business you have established bring in the funds to feed and educate them without you around. Oh why, why do you have to go? Why did you leave so suddenly?

'I am older than you. At 47 years of age you are gone. You have so much more to give, so much to live for, the whole community knew of your ability, your business acumen. Must we lose our foremost migrant leader ...' Elder uncle Chan's voice cracked as he sobbed aloud. He could not continue. He had done well to have said what he did.

Following elder uncle Chan's eulogy, another figure stepped forward. He was a short man, also in the men's Chinese long gown, worn to pay respect to Zhang Yu. It was Peet Xian Sheng, regarded in the Shanghainese community as the English expert. He was often sought as a special interpreter in the High Court whenever there was a case involving a Shanghainese or when a Mandarin speaker was required. He was the manager of the Teck Cheong Shanghai Furniture Co, which did business with the westerners, the British in particular.

He called out: 'Brother Zhang Yu, I am here to say a sad goodbye to you. Why do you have to leave us? We were all so happy together. Our businesses were all doing so well. It will

44

be hard to find someone like you. I bid you goodbye. I salute you for the last time and say a final farewell to my good friend.'

As he finished a shrill cry came from afar. A small lady finally appeared in a traditional long Chinese dress. On reaching the door of the shop she dropped to her knees and crept in on all fours. She shouted 'I can only crawl to you, for you are a god to me. My husband died in an accident, leaving me with three young children. I had no means of support, as I have no relatives in this new country. You saved us, we would have died without you. You gave me enough funds to feed the children and to start a little stall so I could manage a small business and survive. I would gladly die for you if I could. Why do good people like you have to die so early?'

The scene and the words spoken were burnt into Li's memory. Li remembers, too, the sight of Zhang Yu's body being brought home from the hospital. The pitiful cries that greeted it. The shrill 'Law Pere, Law Pere, why did you leave us?' It was MahMah's name for her husband, meaning "boss" in Shanghainese. Her cries were thick with grief. Ah Chieh's cries were softer and gentler, but her grief was no less, for here was the father of her three children. She called him by the same name. Both wives were united in their grief, for both loved him deeply. A sort of bond seemed to have grown between the two women. Ah Chieh was not capable of grudges.

This was also a traumatic time for Li, who could read the pain on Ah Chieh face. When Ah Chieh cried, Li also cried and stayed next to her, refusing to allow the housemaids to drag her away. Ah Chieh told them to leave Li alone. Li was like a little tigress guarding Ah Chieh, glaring at anyone who came near.

The other children were also sobbing. They seemed to know that Zhang Yu had gone forever, for they caught the grief of the adults. I remember Meng sobbing unceasingly. Kwok's face was wet and so was Yeh's.

Nobody was able to sleep that first night. Perhaps little naps from exhaustion. Ah Chieh sat next to the burner placed in front of the coffin. She was constantly feeding the burner with the special paper money bought from the shop that sold paraphernalia for the dead. The paper money was going into the next world so that Zhang Yu had the funds when he arrived there. That was the belief of the Chinese Buddhists. Li sat there also, doing what Ah Chieh did. MahMah often went back to her room upstairs to rest.

The Buddhist ceremony: The monks at their prayers

Tok, tok, tok, a monk started to tap a small wooden boxlike contraption. It is nighttime and the soft sound travelled through the night. It was about nine pm and the shops had closed at seven.

Following the tapping, the chanting of the monks started. It was a slow chant intoned by some six monks and their leader. The monks were shaven young Chinese men in saffron robes, led by an older monk wearing a headdress and an elaborate outer robe. They were chanting the sutras for the dead, very softly at first, but getting a little louder as they continued. It had a soothing effect and seemed to hold everyone in their place.

This was the first night. There were many mourners in the shop: relatives, family friends, members of the Shanghainese community and curious neighbours from nearby.

The monks rose from their seats, thumbing their prayer beads as they chanted. The chief monk led them towards the coffin. They walked around the coffin three times and finally turned to face the coffin, bowing to Zhang Yu's body. By now the chanting had risen to a crescendo and then the volume dropped. It became softer and softer as the monks returned to their seats. As the chanting stopped the tapping began again. Tok, tok, tok. Then it was silent again.

Two hours later the monks started anew. They repeated the earlier performance, but this time the chief monk produced a bell that he rang as he moved. When the prayers were completed the monks retired for the night to a temporary extension with bunks built at the back of the house.

It was a subdued crowd that left the shop. The monks' prayers seemed to have left a certain peace behind, a feeling of calm.

The monks only appeared at night, repeating the chanting of the sutras. Meanwhile a troupe of Buddhist nuns with shaved heads appeared. Dressed in grey, they chanted sutras while counting their prayer beads. One went directly to the kitchen to check on the vegetarian lunch that was to be prepared for them. By late afternoon they were gone.

Zhang Yu and MahMah were not religious. Neither was Ah Chieh, but Ah Heng, the most senior and important of the servants, was. She was the one who looked after the altars, had seen to the lighting of the incense every morning and evening and the display of food and wine to the gods on festivals. MahMah supported all these activities as there was no harm, but rather benefits to be gained by having the gods on the side of the Zhang family. Ah Heng was the one who impressed on MahMah that, because of Zhang Yu's sudden and unexpected death, she must do all she could to pacify Zhang Yu's soul. Which man would leave this mortal world willingly when his children were so young? The monks' prayers were a must, the expense was a necessity. While most well-to-do Chinese had one grand funeral, MahMah decided on three evenings of prayers and a grand funeral.

MahMah always loved showing off. Always full of self-importance, she did not keep an eye on the expenses. The lavish funeral, feeding the monks and mourners, treating the neighbours, ang pows (small cash presents) for those who came to pay their respects to Zhang Yu, were to add up and cost far too much!

There was much noise and movement over the four days while Zhang Yu lay with unseeing eyes. It would have been a fun time had it not been his funeral. This was Li's first exposure to a Buddhist ceremony. True, Li had been to the temple with Ah Heng often. She had held large incense sticks and red joss sticks at the temple and the small incense sticks at home. She had learnt to pray and bow to the gods. She had also learnt to kow tow, to bump her forehead on the floor until it hurt, asking the gods to bless the Zhang family.

According to local Buddhist belief, Zhang Yu had a long journey across the river of the dead to the next world. The monks chanting of the sutras would hasten and smooth this journey. It would also reduce the pain for his loved ones after his sudden exit from this world.

So many deliveries arrived at the shop over the days before the coffin left the shop. Each morning came boxes of fresh vegetables to be cooked for the monks' meals. One afternoon there was a special delivery of model cars, boats, aeroplanes and household items, all made of paper. There were beds, standing fans, crockery and even suitcases! In addition to the paper money burnt by Ah Chieh, these items were to be burnt to arrive in the next world before Zhang Yu did.

It was a fascinating time for Li as she wandered through the dimly lit shop with the dark wood coffin in it. The smell of the flowers was overwhelming, for there were wreaths, large and small, everywhere. To this day the strong smell of flowers takes Li back to this scene. A large photograph of Zhang Yu, mounted in front of his coffin, is embedded in Li's memory.

The paper models intrigued Li. There were also pieces of cotton material mounted as banners, gifts from business friends. Later they were made into clothes for the Zhang family.

The actual day of the funeral was the fourth morning after the body came home.

The household was up early and there was much noise and movement. The coffin was loaded onto some sort of open truck with the wreaths arranged all around it and Zhang Yu's photograph in front. Zhang Yu's last ride. He had moved there in 1932. It had been a seventeen year sojourn.

At the head of the procession were the two widows and Zhang Yu's three young children attended by Ah Heng and two housemaids. They were followed by Li's eldest brother Kwok and sister Meng, for they were the children given to him and MahMah. Then came the other relatives. Zhang Yu had some distant family in Malaya and they all came to the funeral. The immediate family wore jute over their white funeral clothes. Each male wore a white band across his forehead. Yeh and I wore black. The funeral clothes had been prepared at the drop of a hat by the staff of the Shanghai Dressmaking Co!

The funeral cortège moved down Batu Road towards Mountbatten Road and stopped at the junction. There the family and relatives got into cars to continue the journey to the graveyard. The procession had been a hundred people strong up to that point. Li was considered too young and unimportant and was sent home. Alas, there is no record of what happened at the cemetery.

It was an unhappy Li who went back to the shop with the housemaid Lili. There were a few workers there and some neighbouring children still devouring the cakes and fruits send by friends of the family. Li glared at them. They and their parents had turned up to feast on the free food during the days of the wake! The Zhang family had been most generous. MahMah had given permission to order many items as were necessary. Her weakness was a love of show, wanting

49

everything and the best in quality. PaPa would never have allowed such extravagance. He was generous, but still managed money with aplomb!

Steadily, the stash of savings that Zhang Yu kept in the bedroom disappeared. Both the shops had been closed for a week of mourning. There was no income but the workers had to be fed. The dry cleaning shop kicked back to life but activity in the dressmaking shop was painfully slow. Zhang Yu was the dressmaking company. Without him there was no one to hold onto the experts, no one to organise the window displays, no one to import merchandise.

Life was never the same again. The energy was gone, listlessness left in its place. In the months that followed the adults would sometimes weep, while Meng, Yeh and Li presented sad faces. The three children of Ah Chieh were sad and quiet. Li often played with them, for she continued to follow Ah Chieh around. And, over the year after Zhang Yu's death, the shifus left the dressmaking company to start their own dressmaking shops.

The migrants' contribution

The combined skills and contributions of the migrant workers were showcased for Zhang Yu's funeral. The migrants were responsible for its smoothness and success. The young, able-bodied workers from the dry cleaning shop had provided the labour. They moved the sewing machines and the glass display cases from the dressmaking shop to the dry cleaning shop next door. They converted the dressmaking shop into a huge funeral parlour. The migrant dressmakers produced the funeral clothes in no time.

Preparation of the platform and ice baths for Zhang Yu was all done by these migrants. They had no qualms about touching a dead body. They worked with respect and affection for their employer.

Another group of migrants from Ningbo, the workers of elder uncle Chan at the Teck Cheong Shanghai Furniture Company, were responsible for the many chairs sent over to seat the mourners. With their skill they also erected the temporary extension at the back to house the monks. They sought no payment, but a proud MahMah insisted on giving them ang pows. It was the Zhang family style to reward those who helped them.

When the migrants got together, Shanghainese or from neighbouring Ningbo, there was nothing they could not do!

Growing up in a shophouse: late 1940s and early 1950s

Li was a happy child until she was a little over six, as MahMah did not cane her until then. From that time onwards she learnt pain and fear. There were consolations, for as children we learn to make our own happiness. Li's unhappiest years were between the ages of 8 and 10, as she was often punished and miserable. But it was also during those years that she discovered the wonderland around me. Li started to explore her environment around the shop in Batu Road and the nearby streets. Batu Road did not disappoint the curious child that she was.

The Odeon Cinema was a stone's throw from the shop and opened up a whole new world to her. As I told sister Meng, Li saw Johnny Weissmuller in *Tarzan Finds a Son!* six times. There was Esther Williams in her swimming movies. At night, in bed Li would do the backstroke, throwing each arm backwards, just as she had seen Williams do. Years later, when Li finally learnt to swim, it was the backstroke that came naturally to her.

The Odeon Cinema in 1953

As nobody kept an eye on her, Li started venturing out at night. She loved the breeze and the night air. The moonlit nights were beautiful. Somehow, even the dark starless nights had their appeal. On her walk towards Campbell Road Li would hear the chorus of frogs rising to a crescendo as she reached a little bridge. The light rain did not deter me, as she liked the little drops of water on her face. In later years I marvelled at how peaceful life was in this neighbourhood; a young girl going on her walkabout, yet never attacked or molested.

The other magical thing about Batu Road was the nearby food paradise. Li had her allowance from the shop and was not food deprived. In the morning it was the breakfast stalls, at night it was the supper stalls along Campbell Road. If she ventured further Li would reach Kampong Bahru, which was a Malay area. On Sunday nights there was the Pasar Malam, the night market where the stores were all brightly lit. Her favourite stall was run by two middle-aged ladies. They sat on stools behind a big wok, deep frying bananas, sweet potato and yam slices. Li would walk up to the plumper lady, handing her five cents and she never failed to give Li one of the larger pieces of fried yam. Li would muster up her sweetest smile in return for her generosity. Once, in her greedy haste, Li bit too soon into the yam instead of letting it cool and slightly burnt her lips.

Li's other favourite stall was the Malay cake stall, where she bought five cents of "ondai ondai", a green rice flour ball rolled in freshly grated coconut. You put the whole little ball into your mouth, where the brown liquid sugar exploded when you bit into it. It was bliss for those who loved the brown sugar, Gula Malacca.

The breakfast stalls on Campbell Road were open from 6:30 am to 8:30 am.

Li's favourite was the congee stall. The soup must have boiled for many hours with pork and chicken bones. It had minuscule bits of meat and pork innards. Sprinkled on top were small pieces of spring onions and fried onions and drops of garlic oil. It was there that Li had her first lesson on female anatomy.

As Li sat on the stool enjoying the congee, the female hawker drew up her Chinese blouse, pulled out a large, green-veined breast with one hand and swept a little child onto her lap with the other, proceeding to breastfeed the child. Li stared in fascination.

She had never seen a naked breast, and a large one at that!

Serenade of the hawkers

It was not just the stalls, but the roving hawkers who came along Batu Road that made the place fascinating. Each day at sunset the serenade of the hawkers would begin.

'Ai di da ah dia dia,

… Ai dia dia.'

This lilting sad tune haunts me some seventy years later. Apparently the female hawker who sang it had migrated from a remote village near Canton, in south China. She could not speak proper Cantonese. She sang out in her village dialect that she was selling rice bundles filled with a piece of pork, a piece of mushroom and, occasionally, a small chestnut. These rice bundles were known as "choong" in Cantonese and "kwei chang" in the Hokkien dialect. Li found them too filling for supper, while sister Meng liked them. But each night Li would listen for her song.

There was the wonton mee hawker, who would appear not much later. He made a "tok tok" sound as he clattered two pieces of bamboo together. He was brother Kwok's favourite. He could eat whatever he wanted, for MahMah gave him extra pocket money.

The daytime hawkers also appealed to Li, as they sold sweet things. Her favourite was the ice cream man, who would come in the early afternoon before her afternoon nap. He rode a bicycle and rang a little bell as he cycled along.

He carried a large metal box behind him. In the box was dry ice and homemade ice cream, which came in long rolls, much like the modern popsicles. The red bean was the most popular, then came the green bean, followed by the red syrup flavour. Durian was preferred when it was in season.

There was also an exciting gambling game that came with the purchase of the ice cream.

Attached to the metal box was a spinning wheel with numbers on it, similar to a darts board. The highest number was nine, with lots of ones and twos. There were a couple of threes and fours and a solitary five. The nine occupied the smallest space on the board. Li would close her eyes and spin the wheel, happy to get a two. The ice cream seller would proceed to cut two decent sized pieces of ice cream for her. Then one day Li hit the jackpot. The young hawker was downcast, although he cut her nine pieces of ice cream, which, of course, were smaller than the usual size. Li was jubilant and did not mind the size.

Each day she listened for the sound of the bell. It was always a mad dash down the flights of steps, bursting through the back door and down the back lane.

There were other hawkers Li pursued, including the rock candy hawker on his bicycle. The two metal blades he used to chip loose the rock candy from his tray made a "ting ting" sound and Li learnt to listen for it. Often when the hawker chipped at the candy, she would close her eyes, praying 'One more piece, please.' Her pursuit of the hawkers helped Li to develop strong legs and enjoy running. She became good at the 50 and 100 yard sprints in school.

One time during the rainy season Li slipped and fell into a pothole, dirtying her clothes. The punishment was only two strokes of the cane – exaggerated cries of pain got her off lightly. There was no way Li would stop pursuing hawkers. Her love affair with food was just too strong.

Li always felt at home with hawkers. The hawkers in their old and torn clothes were fair. Even as an adult she found she always got the best when she bought fruit, for the sellers were her friends.

Growing up in Batu Road Li also learnt multiculturism. From the young Indian boys who worked at the Odeon Cinema she received kindness, including free entry. It was an Indian boy who came to help her when she was knocked down by a motorcycle at the age of nine. A kind Malay lady at the Sunday night market at the nearby kampong always gave her good value for money.

Li considered herself lucky that she grew up in Batu Road.

Li's neighbourhood: Growing up on Batu Road

Looking back, Li regard herself as very lucky, for she lived in a wonderland. The upside of being neglected was to enjoy so much freedom. There was not just her nocturnal roaming, but her early morning outings in the early 1950s. Ah Chieh left the Zhang family in early 1951. Li had searched for and found her. Nobody else knew about it. It was her secret and Li hid it well. Li certainly did not want MahMah to find out and stop her from seeing Ah Chieh.

In late 1951 Li was eleven, tanned and scrawny. She was up and out of the house as the sky brightened, on her way to the common source of transport, the trishaw. It was only 20 minutes' walk to where the trishaw riders and pullers congregated for their breakfast. At this stall they knelt on the benches, consuming large bowls of congee. Li would find herself a stool, sit and wait patiently for one of them to finish breakfast and take her Jalan Linai, the road where Ah Chieh lived when she was in Kuala Lumpur. If Ah Chieh was out her mother, PorPor See, would be there, as her bound feet kept her home. PorPor See would pay Li's fare and feed her with biscuits.

Li loved the trishaw rides in the early mornings. The trishaw rider would go quite fast, as he was fresh and Li, the first passenger of the day, weighed little. Besides, at that hour there was hardly any traffic. It was a beautiful ride as Li sped past the shophouses, the cool breeze on her face, leaving the town for the lush green countryside at 6:15 in the morning. It was not surprising that Li took to skiing in later life, for there was more of that exhilaration. The ride must have taken more than a half hour and cost a handsome 80 cents.

The trishaw riders were always tanned and skinny with well-muscled legs. They were often in their late twenties or mid-thirties, always Chinese. They were polite and Li trusted them. Perhaps it was too early for them to be cranky. Li's wonderland was certainly a peaceful one.

Nearby shops were also part of her world. Just a few doors away from the shophouse, the Selangor Pewter Co was starting to establish itself. A pleasant couple brought items from their factory to the shop every morning,. The wife would often talk to Li. Her husband's forebears had started the business. They had three children, two girls and a boy. Li met the younger sister at the Victoria Institution, but the elder girl went to a different school. Li met her in a combined science class.

Then there was her favourite candy shop. It was really a provision shop that sold almost everything one could think of. For the young Li it was the wide range of candies that mattered. It was family-run. The father was a handsome man who was always working, hauling sacks of rice, crockery, house cleaning utensils, etc. He was the honest man who gave the seven year old Li correct change from the ten dollar note with the hole in the centre. Li was to meet someone who looked so much like him selling cloisonné ornaments along the Great Wall of China half a century later.

His small little wife was also always working. Li would see them leaving their bowls of rice and vegetables to attend to customers. Their six young sons helped in the shop. The eldest, Ah Huai, was the favourite of Li and her siblings, as he was the most generous with the amount of candy he handed out for their five cents. The next two brothers would sometimes shortchange them!

It was at this shop that Li spent many of her happy moments as a child. Sometimes she would stand in front of the Chinese candy jars, taking her time to decide what she would like. The speed of her decision depended on how much money she had. Sometimes Ah Chieh would give her an extra five or ten cents. Occasionally, a Shanghainese visitor would give the Zhang children some lolly money.

One top choice of the Zhang children was sweetened dried plums chopped into small pieces. It had the unsavoury name of Yong mare see, which in the Cantonese dialect means goat's droppings! On days when Li had only five cents her choice would be the sour plums, as these were cheaper and lasted longer, nine sour plums compared to three sweet olives for five cents that Li also loved.

And finally was the Indian shop at the end of the row of shops to the right, immediately opposite the Odeon Theatre. It was a simple restaurant, continuously playing songs in Hindi. Kwok and Meng would send Li there to buy a bowl of lamb curry for thirty cents. The Zhang siblings learnt to eat spicy food early in their childhood. Li learnt to count up to ten in Hindi and some Hindi songs, or rather, parts of Hindi songs. Whenever she wanted to ingratiate herself with the Indians, who were largely Hindu, she would count or sing in Hindi. Most times it was both. It never failed to amuse them and often she was rewarded with Indian sweets.

New clothes for Chinese New Year

Li knows Chinese New Year is approaching and she is filled with anxiety and impatience. It relates to her new dresses. Besides food, she loves new clothes. Since she was five Li receives three new dresses the week before every Chinese New Year.

Ah Chieh is in charge and Li follows her to look at the bales of cloth in the shop. Ah Chieh searches through and removes only pieces that are less than a yard long. Li is small, adding a bit of height each year but not weight. It does not matter to her that Ah Chieh is economising.

'Oh, this piece of material has less than half a yard left, but it was expensive. It may be insufficient to sew a whole dress for you. I will find a matching material for a skirt,' says Ah Chieh. Li claps her hand in glee, for she loves the bright colours of the material. Ah Chieh finds another small piece and again searches for another piece to match it. Ah Chieh has good taste. The materials combine well and two dresses are well-matched. The third dress is of a single material, and is pretty.

Li sits in the workroom, watching the seamstress sew one of her new dresses. The housemaid has to drag her to her afternoon nap. Li is told that it may be completed when she returns after her nap. The seamstress has just started on the sleeves. Li rushes down after the nap. Joy oh joy, she finds that the dress has just been finished.

This goes on until Li is eleven years of age. At thirteen, Ah Chieh is gone but Li is still able to wear two of the dresses Ah Chieh chose. Li quietly hopes that she will not outgrow them. They remind her of Ah Chieh.

A love so pure: Li and Ah Chieh

A child's love is so beautiful, yet adults do not always recognise it. The child does not discriminate, makes no demands. Love transcends colour and blood ties. A child gives freely. It is unconditional love, it is spontaneous, it is pure love at its best. Li at three accepts love from anybody who is willing to give it to her. It does not have to be a relative.

Little Li's hugs are not fleeting. Ah Chieh found it amusing the first time, remarking to a friend 'If little Li likes you she hugs you real hard with her little body until she gives a shudder, and only then she lets you go. She is a very loving child.'

Li's love is forever. Here is a scene of Li at seven. She had been sent back to her mother for some weeks and was unwell. Ah Chieh heard about it and went to the Imbi Road house to see her. Luk May greeted Ah Chieh and took her into the room where Li lay on a bed.

Li's eyes lit up when she saw Ah Chieh. By this time Li had been told that love and care can only be given by one's own mother. She had loved Ah Chieh since she was three. Now in the presence of Luk May and Ah Chieh she was confused. Both the women looked at her. The corners of Li's lips drooped, then quivered, and next she burst into tears. The two women watched Li and burst out laughing.

Luk May never looked at Li the way Ah Chieh did. Luk May's smile was reserved for Mei, Sang and Chien. Luk May never held Li's fingers like Ah Chieh did. Still, Li felt guilty, for Ah Chieh was the one she loved and she was not her mother. For Li love came spontaneously. She would love MahMah too had she been allowed to.

As an adult at nineteen years of age Li learnt to love Kit and his father KM. To Grace, love was reserved for those most closely related by blood and Li did not have the right to love her men. But Li knew something Grace did not; that love has no boundaries. Li loved Kit as a soul mate and KM as a father. Grace doubted her love could be genuine, or that Li was capable of real affection. Besides which, Li was not deserving or good enough. Both Kit's sister and mother doubted Li's true feelings! And Li had done the unforgivable: she had made both men love her.

In her teens, Li was told that Ah Chieh had only showed fondness and played with her because she had time on her hands. PaPa was always busy and she did not want to face MahMah, the senior wife, who often frowned and was regularly cranky. It was true that when Ah Chieh became a mother she had little time for Li, but Ah Chieh always smiled at her. Whatever love she gave Li went a long way and it was at a time when Li needed love. To Li, Ah Chieh was the most beautiful and wonderful person in the world. The adult Li remembered that Little Li was always looking for Ah Chieh, just to gaze at the beloved face. Li did feel jealousy over Ah Chieh's children, but she learnt to love them too, for they were Ah Chieh's children. Ah Chieh was the person Li loved the most until Kit.

I can recall only one occasion when Ah Chieh reprimanded little Li. Li was six and had wanted to go out to play. It was getting dark and Li was annoyed when Ah Chieh said no to her. Li had muttered softly 'Say Ah Chieh, say Ah Chieh.' She had learnt it from the housemaids. "Say" meant dead. The housemaids used the word often, saying "say loh" referring to a man and "say por" about a woman if they were annoyed. Ah Chieh only said 'I heard you, you naughty girl.' That was the end of the matter.

In my whole life, I feel the saddest person, the one that life treated most harshly, was Ah Chieh. She was truly a beautiful person, gentle, kind and forgiving. Sold as a child of twelve by an unscrupulous uncle, she had to adapt to a new life. She trained day and night in acrobatics, singing and acting to become a performer in the Peking Opera. Part of the training included cooking famous Peking dishes. She also learnt to sew and do housework. As a teenager she additionally had to learn to care for the two sisters her foster mother adopted. Her marriage to Zhang Yu was not really a free choice, but was agreed as she had three dependants to think of.

Ah Chieh's marriage of five years did give her some happiness. She and Zhang Yu fell in love. Little Li saw them hugging when they thought no one was watching. She had to share her husband with the very difficult and temperamental older woman who had selected her. She had to watch her step all the time, never giving offence, but remaining submissive and docile. The slightest offence, imagined or accidental, would lead to a big argument between Zhang Yu and senior wife Foong Ying. At social functions, Ah Chieh would stay quiet while Foong Ying would brag.

The birth of each child was officially registered showing Zhang Foong Ying as the mother and Zhang Yu as the father. Ah Chieh had no rights. Zhang Yu's death brought her more suffering.

Luckily, by 1949 Ah Chieh's sisters were no longer dependants. Lao Er had returned to Shanghai, while Lao San had turned out to be a good hairdresser and married. Only her old mother, PorPor See, was left with her at the shop.

Without Zhang Yu the dressmaking shop went downhill. PorPor's allowance disappeared. The small sums of cash Ah Chieh was given to spend as she wished or remit to Shanghai also vanished. Only the dry cleaning shop kept the Zhang family afloat. MahMah kept the accounts for both shops but she had no dressmaking or business skills. Still, no one could out-argue or out-curse her.

MahMah gave Ah Chieh a small allowance, but she had to spend long hours 'minding' the shop. From that small allowance, Ah Chieh gave PorPor money for cigarettes and coffee. Meanwhile, MahMah increasingly turned to opium.

When night came and she was alone, Ah Chieh wept. There was no breadwinner to look after her. She was not yet 30 years of age and was tied down to three young children.

Ah Chieh received advice from MahMah's friend Hilda and sister Lao San: 'Go. Leave this unhappy place.'

Ah Chieh had a quiet, calm beauty, and was still attractive. She was still desirable as a concubine or junior wife to a rich man. At least she would have more money to spend and provide a more comfortable living for her mother, with no worries over cigarettes and coffee. Indeed, there had been "feelers", for there were rich middle-aged Chinese businessmen who had heard of this Shanghai beauty.

It was in 1951 when Ah Chieh made the decision to go, leaving the Zhang family for good. One morning, as soon as senior clerk, Mr Wong, from the dry cleaning shop arrived, Ah Chieh went up to him. She handed him a heavy bunch of keys, instructing him to give them to MahMah when she came down to the shop. The latter always slept until mid-morning. Ah Chieh muttered that she had something urgent to deal with, Mr Wong told me later. Then she was gone, never to return to the shop again.

That fateful day, 11 year old Li came home to find that something was wrong. There was an eerie silence. Then came a shrill wail from the master bedroom. It was MahMah's voice as she called her husband's name.

'Law pere, law pere, she is trash. She cannot run away. We are a respectable family'. The words were punctuated by sobs. MahMah was lying in bed as if she were sick. Li was confused, not knowing what had happened.

The bombshell came as Li was eating. Sister Meng said that Ah Chieh had run away, taking her mother and two younger children. She had gone to Penang to marry PaPa's old friend and would never come back. Li choked on her rice, dropped her bowl and chopsticks and ran to her bedroom, tears flowing fast and furious.

Meng said Ah Chieh would never return. She now belonged to another family. Li's heart was breaking, she wanted to die. This is the first time Li went to "dark places". She was in pain. Blackness surrounded her and there was only emptiness. This was the first time Li felt such so much despair.

What are dark places? Can it be described? There is darkness and despair, tinged with unhappiness and self-doubt. There is emptiness and pain. It is like a vast endless desert. All one sees is nothingness. One feels depression, loss of hope and emptiness. There is no one to turn to, no one to love and no purpose to existence. Li was too young to know enough of life. The one person who would smile at her, Ah Chieh, was gone, and there was no one to relate to. There was no meaning to life, just emptiness and misery.

MahMah took to her bed for the next two days. The Shanghainese women in the Zhang family did not play-act with their emotions. I think that MahMah did have some kind of affection for Ah Chieh, and a strange attachment had grown between the two women. I remember my friend Dee's mother from Teck Cheong Shanghai Furniture Co visiting and trying to console MahMah.

I feel compelled to tell the rest of Ah Chieh's story.

I related in my earlier book that Li found Ah Chieh some six months later. Ah Chieh's sufferings did not end. She was accused of having unlawfully kidnapped the two younger children and had to surrender them to MahMah, their official mother, a few months later. Besides, MahMah argued, if she had to be travelling with her new husband how was she going to handle the children's education? Ah Chieh returned them to the Zhang family.

She had lost a husband she had learnt to love for the short time they were married. She now married again according to Chinese rites. It was not for love, but because of the need to survive. She owed filial piety to her mother, who would live better.

There was no happiness for Ah Chieh. There was always pain, for she had to live without her little ones. I met her about three times the next year. She always gave me her beautiful smile but I could sense her longing for her children. I felt she had dedicated herself to her husband's business and kept herself busy to stop her mind from drifting to her children.

Ah Chieh lived for the times she returned to Kuala Lumpur and saw her children. Ah Heng included me in two of the lunchtime meetings, arranged by a mutual friend. They had to make the meetings lucrative for MahMah. Her opium habit was expensive and only one shop was managing well. Ah Chieh gave whatever money she could. I continued to secretly meet her. She always paid my trishaw fare, plus something extra for my lolly money.

I heard that life was passable for her the first few years. She moved to Hong Kong and stopped travelling with her husband. It was from Hong Kong that she returned to Malaysia some twelve years later, when her boys called her home. She had been away seventeen years. The boys had suffered, but grew up to be intelligent and successful. Ah Chieh was to receive some happiness once more; she got to enjoy her grandchildren. MahMah was the lucky one, though, for Ah Chieh threw herself into looking after her, making all her favourite dishes. Almost every day MahMah enjoyed glutinous rice balls. When MahMah became bedridden and weak from her advanced opium addiction, it was Ah Chieh who bathed, massaged and spoon-fed her.

The canings

Prior to the age of six, when the caning started, I had not experienced physical pain or fear. I do not know when it began for Yeh. The first year of caning was not so bad for me. Then the frequency and ferocity increased. I think the worst year was when Zhang Yu passed away when I was nine. Perhaps MahMah was in great pain and needed to pass it on. She told Yeh and me that we were such bad children we had caused the stress that led to his death. I believed her and told Yeh that we must be good lest we caused her death too! Who would look after us if that happened?

I remember one special caning session in the year Zhang Yu passed away. I had my usual punishment. Then it was Yeh's turn. I watched MahMah land the cane on Yeh's legs. I suddenly noticed that she seemed to be working herself into a frenzy. She had a glint in her eye as she hit Yeh. Was she getting a high from it? Was it similar to the kick she got from her opium hit?

Ah Heng had taken a strong dislike to Yeh and sometimes stayed to watch the caning.

I remember Ah Heng complaining to MahMah that the canes were splitting and needed to be replaced. At this MahMah had exclaimed that these two children had such thick skins!

At nine Li could think 'No, MahMah, our skins are not extra thick. It is your intensity and strength, especially for Yeh.' It occurred to Li that this was the only exercise MahMah had – a release for her by causing physical and mental pain to two children. For Li, being called a prostitute was more painful than Yeh felt at being called a robber. Yet Li retained her sense of humour, for whenever MahMah said she would write her name upside-down if anything good came out of these two children,

Li would think 'Would it not be easier for MahMah to write her name in Chinese and then turn the paper upside down?'

Ah Chieh had learnt early not to interfere with the caning or anything else. It would have been at her own peril, for interference was incitement for MahMah to do worse. You did not want to see MahMah in full fury. Ah Chieh kept herself well away from such scenes.

As I've said, I never hated MahMah, for I did not know how to hate, but as an adult I wondered why she mistreated Yeh and me. Meng had not been caned, although she was often sworn at. Mei, Sang and Chien were with our parents and were spared the treatment. The caning had ended by the time they returned to the shop in 1953. MahMah had aged and no longer had the energy for it.

What demons rode on MahMah's back? How could she love Weng and brother Kwok and treat Yeh and me badly? She swore and cursed each time she caned us, and I was beginning to be convinced that I needed to be beaten to make me good.

I wonder whether there is a flaw in humans that makes them pick on others. Must scapegoats be made of those who are unable to retaliate, children in particular? Do victimisers not realise that they can damage children psychologically, make them think there is something badly wrong with them? Probably they do not care. Yeh was a beautiful child. With his gentle face one wonders why he would be picked on. Li had those provocative intense eyes, a child more likely to be disliked, but why Yeh?

The Journey

The shadows are all around me

I cannot see,

Where am I?

Am I in an abyss?

Why is it so dark?

Help me, somebody please help me.

I need to get up from where I am lying,

I need to get out but I cannot see.

I crawl around but it is the same in every direction.

Wait, there is a dim light

So small, I can hardly see but

I crawl towards it.

It is somewhere I can move towards

In this vast darkness.

As I move in its direction

It brightens, but ever so slightly.

Yet it is still too far.

I am tired, I want to sleep.

Sideways, backwards I move,

It seems so much easier for me

to lie down and rest.

But something compels me to move on

Yet it is far away.

Do I hear a soft faint music, as if made by a wind
instrument?

It lifts my soul and so I crawl on.

I drag my weary body, it seems for ages.

Then suddenly I can see.

A scene of beauty,

Of lush green trees, flowers, a pool, a waterfall.

No more darkness, but a subdued light.

There is a gentle breeze, freshness,

I feel serenity, peace,

Have I completed my journey?

The Rise and Fall of the Zhang Family Fortunes

The Zhang family business had been well planned and the timing was almost perfect. Zhang Yu established the first large dressmaking shop in Malaya in 1932. It was THE dressmaking shop by the 1940s. Any young lady who was the daughter of somebody important demanded to have her wedding dress made there. Zhang Yu had worked day and night to establish this business. He was no devious, unscrupulous business man, but an honest person profiting from his own work, realising his dream of bringing fashion to Malaya from Shanghai.

The Shanghai Dressmaking Co shop stood on Batu Road with stunning dresses in both shop windows. In one was a western-style wedding dress with matching accessories. In the latter half of the 1940s the wedding dresses were changed monthly, so people would come especially to see them. In the other window was an attractive western evening dress of the latest fashion. Every now and then a long sequinned cheongsam would appear. Only one business rivalled the Zhang business – the larger British-owned Robinson's, a department store that did more than fashion. However, Robinson's sold English goods, was expensive and catered for the English and European woman, while the Shanghai Dressmaking Co was for the well-to-do local Chinese woman. The population in Kuala Lumpur was largely Chinese. Of course, Zhang Yu hoped to attract the "white woman" and the western-educated Chinese female to his western dresses.

Zhang Yu brought the tight fitting, figure hugging, sexy cheongsam, which had made its appearance in Shanghai, to the Shanghai Dressmaking Co. The older Chinese women clung to the loose fitting version, but the young and the bold preferred the new.

The Shanghai Dressmaking Co and Zhang Yu

After the end of World War II Kuala Lumpur was humming with brisk activity. The commercial centre was alive again and so were the two shops – the Shanghai Dressmaking Co and OIC (Oriental International and Cleaning), the dry cleaning company – with Zhang Yu at the helm.

It was 1946 and Britain resumed its role as a top colonial power. British efficiency and British supremacy were fully re-established. The English schools were reopened, the Union Jack flew at all the large buildings, and *God Save the King* was heard in the schools and clubs and at all official and social gatherings. Little Li was learning to hum the tune. The Japanese occupation was a thing of the past. Did it really happen?

As the British flourished in the next couple of years, so did the Zhang family business.

Li recalls those years.

The Shanghai Dressmaking Co stood out in Batu Road. The two front windows of the shop displayed the most exquisite dresses, a wedding dress in one and a western evening dress in the other. Zhang Yu succeeded in attracting a western clientele. The wives of the top army officers found they did not have to wait to return to UK to have their evening dresses made, for there was the Shanghai Dressmaking Co, which had little Chinamen who cut and sewed beautifully. These tailors were trained in Shanghai. The dresses fitted better and were much cheaper than those bought in London. The English ladies could have as many fitting sessions as they wanted. They could find attractive and expensive materials in the shop as well. Zhang Yu had the materials imported from Shanghai and some had their origins in Paris. There were fashion books that Zhang Yu expensively paid for, although they were cast aside after he died. A ten year old little Li found and busily cut them up with a pair of scissors. The pretty cut-outs of fashionable dresses were to be found among Li's school textbooks.

The dry cleaning shop held no attraction for Li, but the Shanghai Dressmaking Co was a magnet. Besides the clothes on display there were so many colourful items, such as the beautiful silk flowers brides always bought for their hair. There were the sequinned and beaded evening bags that Zhang Yu imported from Hong Kong. Next to them were the silk scarves and handkerchiefs. Then there were the jewellery boxes and pretty little vases. Along the walls of the shop were the rolls of imported textiles, colourful and soft evening materials so popular with the English ladies. These rolls of materials were kept on display behind glass.

Towards the back of the shop were three main work areas where the shifus, the experts, sat. The first was the European dress expert, Chung Dee shifu, whose work was the western evening dress. Then there was the cheongsam expert, Chooi shifu, who was becoming very popular, as he was the best cheongsam tailor in the whole of Malaya. A third area was largely for day clothes, suits and well-cut smart dresses for the rich ladies of Kuala Lumpur. Young Ching worked in this area. In fact, there was also an extension where Loke shifu did the men's suits.

Zhang Yu knew enough of dressmaking to get along with the tailors. In Li's memory PaPa could draft, cut and sew beautifully, but was more interested in running the business. Zhang Yu spoke in Shanghainese with his dressmaking shifus.

He treated them well, paid them well and they respected and were content under him. Zhang Yu was the business mind and they left the problems with him.

By early 1949, the Shanghai Dressmaking Co was the undisputed leading dressmaking company in Malaya.

Zhang Yu was well established. He was invited to meetings with other businessmen. He had proved himself. There were ventures that could do with his help and they wanted his ideas. The world of business was at his feet.

Zhang Yu had fulfilled his dream. He had brought fashion to Malaya. What next? A new world of opportunities in a young country lay before him. Certainly he had no thought of death!

One beautiful morning in May 1948

It was closing time and there was great excitement in the dry cleaning shop. It had started the early afternoon. A British officer had come into OIC and asked for the boss. Zhang Yu appeared and was handed a cheque. Cheques were only used for large sums of money and government transactions, everything else was in cash. It was a cheque for the largest sum of money he had ever seen, almost a thousand Malayan dollars. It was payment for the cleaning of carpets, drapes and military uniforms, what the British Army owed OIC, clearing their debt.

Zhang Yu wore a smile. At closing time he wore a bigger one. The cash earnings for the day were also good. This was the biggest daily take for OIC. That was not all, for there was also the takings from the Shanghai Dress Making Co, which brought in a steady income.

Soon the news spread through the two shops. There was laughter coming from the family living quarters upstairs. MahMah was full of smiles and small talk. Ah Chieh beamed and the Zhang children caught the joy. Li clapped and giggled. A normally solemn looking Zhang Yu looked anything but serious! The workers were elated and their voices shrill from the excitement. They knew there would be a feast. Zhang Yu was a good boss. His generosity could be seen in the next day's meals. There were two additional dishes: chicken in white wine with flat rice noodle in pork, and mushrooms with the favourite Shanghainese cabbage wong bak. (Li recalls watching young apprentice Ah Tse slurping what was left of the wine in the chicken dish!) Outstanding takings did not mean bonuses, for that was a Chinese New Year tradition. The size of the bonus depended on the size of the profits for the year. Zhang Yu never took his eye off the accounts. He had a business to run and responsibilities to fulfill.

Respect for Zhang Yu increased even further and one could understand why the younger workers bowed each time they ran into him.

The takings that day could have been invested locally. That sum would have bought a small house or a large piece of land in a respectable area, but Zhang Yu had his priorities. Each month the rent had to be paid and the workers fed and housed. Funds had to be remitted to Shanghai, not only for the purchase of merchandise, but to the families of the young workers. Lastly, but most importantly, profits went to the original investors and their families in Shanghai.

Zhang Yu had also helped to start a local charity under the 'San Kong gong hui', which was the Shanghainese Association. It was to assist needy Shanghainese migrants stranded in Malaya. How did Li know? Li knew because she saw the receipts made out to the Association left for many years under the glass top of Zhang Yu's desk. Zhang Yu was gone but the growing child would look at the papers again and again as she laid her head on the cool glass top.

Yet in 1949, investing locally was also capturing the interest of Chinese businessmen. One person was Zhang Yu's old friend Chan from the Teck Cheong Shanghai Furniture Co. Had Zhang Yu lived perhaps he would have done that too, for local land was so cheap ...

As a teenager Li learnt something about business. With a business like the Zhang family's one could earn an income every day, unlike the wage earner for whom it was fixed and received once a month. Like Zhang Yu, who showed flamboyance, one could afford extravagance too. As a child Li did not know much about being frugal, because she was able to get whatever spending money she wanted, and her clothes were supplied from the dressmaking shop. That these items were of high quality did not occur to Li – they were simply what were available to her. It was a case of being used to expensive clothes rather than extravagance.

Li also felt she inherited some Shanghainese business acumen. IF Zhang Yu had lived longer, IF Li had been older, perhaps she could have helped in the family business. IF …

Management issues

While the dressmaking business was identified with Zhang Yu and slowly collapsed without him, the dry cleaning business was more durable. The latter lasted until around 1960. It kept the family financially afloat.

Had there been someone capable to manage the shops, both the businesses would have survived. It did not need someone as brilliant as Zhang Yu. The groundwork had been done by him. It was such a pity! As little Li grew into a teenager she witnessed the departure of the more capable workers from both the shops. There was no increase in their salaries, no spending on the premises to keep them looking good, only the annual paint job and daily cleaning. To put it bluntly, the person who now had control knew only how to empty the till at the end of the day.

MahMah was aggressive and tough, but she did not have business acumen. She had neither the interest nor the foresight to bring in new merchandise as Zhang Yu had. In 1949, when the new Communist Government was established in China, she allowed the old trade links to Shanghai to collapse. She had no thoughts about ploughing money back into the business. Zhang Yu's cousin, Cheong, who continued as the manager, had little initiative or imagination, and was unwilling to exert himself. He was good only as a follower. Besides he was faced with the formidable MahMah, Zhang Foong Ying.

There was still a future for the dry cleaning business. All it needed was a steady hand at the helm. At that time in Malaya, the cleaning businesses were largely small laundries, with perhaps a boss and two or three workmen, while OIC had more than a dozen workers and more services to offer. It used the latest techniques and cleaning products from Shanghai, besides being able to manage carpets and curtains. No surprise that it caught the eye of the British Army officials and their business.

The money slowly starts to run out

The family funds had been low when Zhang Yu died in 1949, as he had made a short trip to Shanghai the year before, taking his savings with him. In 1948, when Jen returned to Shanghai with Luk May, Mei, Sang and Chien, he, too, had carried savings back to his father. Jen's father had been an original investor and planner of the Zhang family. As part of the family, Jen's sisters also enjoyed benefits. In the late 1930s both Yu and Zen had purchased land in Shanghai. That was the pattern of the family workings: take back savings, return and save again.

MahMah did Jen an injustice when, after Zhang Yu's death, she behaved as if both shops belonged exclusively to her husband. She had allowed Ah Heng to believe that and allowed Ah Heng to call Li and her siblings parasites. Ah Heng had looked after Zhang Yu's eldest son, Weng, from birth, and wanted to believe he was the true heir. She hated Jen, and nicknamed him 'Elephant', for he was a big man and clumsy at times. She could see that Yu was a capable man and did not need Jen's help, which is why Jen could go off to Singapore to start his own business.

Jen never argued with MahMah. She was the daughter of his father's elder brother, and was considerably older than he. Years later, Ah Chieh told me that Jen was the one who cried the most at Yu's funeral. He had, in fact, broken down. Jen respected MahMah, never challenged her and, once he was established in Singapore, took no money from the shops in KL. When MahMah called him back in 1953, saying she needed help to manage the KL shops, he sold his business and put all his funds into the Shanghai Dressmaking Co.

The shop now sold a range of household items. I remember that Jen's favourite item was the new kerosene stove with two burners. But Jen was no salesman and the new business collapsed.

MahMah did more than her share of damage to the family fortunes. In 1949, when Zhang Yu went, she had refused a replacement for him. No one was good enough. She did not want any help from Jen either. Her spendthrift ways and her attitude towards others were damaging. She always knew best. Zhang Yu had been the only one she listened to, and even then she put up a fight.

Some of the seeds of ruin were there at Zhang Yu's funeral, in the mismanagement of the expenses. MahMah spent on a scale unheard of. But she was the matriarch and did as she pleased.

The family funds had always been handled by Zhang Yu. MahMah had everything she wanted, as Yu saw to most things. He never denied her anything, for he never forgot that her father's money had helped him start the business. Even when she started smoking opium he gave her the money. He thought it was just a fun thing. He never thought she would become an addict. Indeed, she was not addicted while he lived.

Zhang Yu kept cash at home because he was always aware that emergencies may arise. He had been through the Japanese occupation. He had his stash of cash in a secret place in his bedroom. He told MahMah where it was, but not Ah Chieh, as he feared she was too kind and vulnerable. Ah Chieh knew, in any case, but pretended to be ignorant, she told me later.

On the second day after Zhang Yu's death, MahMah went to the hiding place and brought out the cash, for she realised there was much spending to be done. She was also aware that the shops had accounts at the bank.

The first demands were the bills for the fresh vegetables delivered every morning to the kitchen. Another priority was the monks and nuns. MahMah gave generous ang pows to the workers from the furniture shop. They had put up the temporary quarters for the monks at the back of the shop, although the work had been voluntary.

The coffin shop asked for cash, and since the coffin was of the best it was costly. Then came the shop that sold all the paraphernalia relating to the dead, the joss sticks of various sizes, the incense, the paper money for the dead, the burners, and so on.

Just days later came the monks' demands for payment, followed by that from the nuns. They cost the most, a small fortune, for they had returned for further prayers 21 days later to appease Yu's soul. Although the other bills were smaller by comparison, it all added up. The paper model shop's bill was no small thing, as MahMah had ordered the whole range, from domestic items to aeroplanes and boats. Food had been ordered for the mourners and those bills had come, too. Did anyone check the bills? What about the three roasted pigs that were ordered for the day of the funeral? In her grief MahMah did not glance at the mounting debts. She only wanted a show and the best for her husband. Zhang Yu would never have approved of the expenses. The road downhill had started.

And so the years passed. Jen's attempt to revive the family fortunes failed, although the shop survived for some years. Manager Cheong left after much nagging from his wife, as it was clear to her there was no future left in the Shanghai Dressmaking Co. The shop was merely breaking even, then, when it was not even doing that, it had to close down.

In 1955 some Shanghainese businessmen, friends of Zhang Yu, stepped in. The shop now sold decorative items, including cheap jade statues and vases for middle class Chinese families. Again, it did not succeed and was turned into a high class shoe shop, financed and run by a Shanghainese businessman. There was a good range of shoes from Hong Kong. It did reasonably well for a year but business slowly turned poor again.

77

Meanwhile, the Zhang children were growing up. In 1956 Li was in Form 4, Mei in Form 5, and Meng was working as a clerk for the Malayan Railways. Jen turned to horse racing and the bookie business.

Sadly, the shop was leased out as a coffee shop. The shop at 219 Batu Road, formerly known as the Shanghai Dressmaking Co, was no more. The connecting stairway was sealed. The Zhang siblings continued to live on the top floor, but they only used the stairs of the dry cleaning shop. It was a much quieter place, a far cry from its heyday when Zhang Yu was alive.

The Story of Kit

While Li was being made in the shophouse in Batu Road, Kit was growing up in the rural towns of Pahang. As a government servant, Kit's father, KM, was transferred to different towns when they needed the services of a court interpreter.

It was a simple, leisurely life as distractions were few, with not even a cinema in some towns.

The many years in these small towns taught Kit the importance of the core family, away from the numerous relatives of KM's brothers and sisters and their families. Kit's elder sister Chun was unusually mature, self-assured and serious. While most Chinese children viewed their fathers with fear, it was never the case with Chun. She could approach him at any time with her numerous questions. From the moment KM held her in his arms he felt she was special. He did her night feeds; his little girl mattered more than his sleep. She was the almost perfect child. She seldom cried and was always practical, tantrums were rare. Kit cried often, whimpered, frequently running to his mother while avoiding the stern looking father. As Kit told Li, he was so afraid of his father that he never sat down to talk to KM until his university years. He was also a late developer physically. Chun was a head taller than him when she was twelve and he was ten. He did not grow tall until he was sixteen. He often suffered colds, while Chun was the happy, healthy laughing child. Kit felt he was a disappointment to his father, while his mother loved him unconditionally.

Humour while in danger

The Japanese Occupation had the effect of pushing families even closer together. Kit was born in 1937. When the Japanese invaded Malaya he was only four. The family was lucky to have in their employ a kindly former "Black and White", Ah Wong, a professional servant who was cook and housekeeper. She had left the sisterhood and married. Ah Wong had a son who was much older than Kit. She left him with relatives when she returned to domestic work, as she needed the funds. I do not know whether her husband died or disappeared. She was devoted to Kit and was a good hard worker. Ah Wong was given the responsibility of Kit's safety during the Japanese occupation while Grace would run and hide with Chun from the Japanese invaders. Rape had become synonymous with Japanese soldiers.

Kit told me that one day in early 1942 the alarm sounded that Japanese soldiers were on the prowl. Ah Wong hid in the undergrowth with Kit.

A young Japanese soldier approached their hiding place. He seemed to be looking for a place to pee when he saw the half-hidden face of this not-too-young woman with a young boy. In fright, Ah Wong jolted up from her crouching position. The sudden movement caused her waist-long hair to jerk loose from its pins and tumble all over her face. The young soldier burst into shrieks of laughter at the sight of the terrified, long-haired woman. He took off, still laughing, well away from Ah Wong and Kit.

Family matters

The year 1942 was one of fear, sorrow and death. The Japanese established the most brutal control. Looters and resistance fighters were decapitated, their heads displayed on spikes. The aim was to reduce the local population into submission. An unfortunate civilian could be shot on the spot or rounded up and never seen again. Some fathers never came home, including the father of brother Kwok's wife!

In the uncertain tumultuous times, when death was no stranger, families grew even closer together. And so it was with Kit's family.

In 1964, KM's sudden death at the age of fifty-three left a deeply bereaved family. Li could sense Kit's feelings of guilt. As a doctor he should have been aware that KM had a heart problem. He was so locked up in his grief that he did not notice the vitriol when Grace's remarked that she should never have allowed Kit to marry Li. He was not aware that Li had been missing for over an hour, on the verge of suicide following Grace's comment, and a second tragedy could have occurred. Li feels it was then that Kit vowed to himself that he would make it up to his mother. He would protect her and cherish her.

The making of the devoted son was finally complete.

The Growing Years: 1950s

The Second World War and the Japanese occupation are things of the past as Malaya recovers financially. Rubber and tin continue to bring wealth to the British, who stand out as the leading colonial masters in South East Asia, leaving France and The Netherlands behind. I recall the former Prime Minister of Singapore, Lee Kwan Yew, saying 'the British have more finesse, they knew when to leave.' The other colonial powers had to be pushed out through uprisings and bloodshed, but not the British. They left peacefully as friends and with fat wallets.

The British interfered as little as possible in the lives of the people of the colonies as long as the profits flowed in. In Malaya, the British made little attempt to try and unite the various races. The indigenous people of the country, the Malays, were left to live their idyllic lives in their rural village kampongs, while the Chinese and Indians did well in the towns. Chinese labour at the tin mines and Indian labour at the rubber estates ensured the flow of revenue to Britain. As the country developed and the population grew, the educated Indians worked in the civil service while the uneducated ones helped to build the roads. The uneducated Chinese swelled the ranks of the Indian rubber tappers at the ever-expanding rubber estates. By this time, the French and other Europeans had also started investing in the country.

Nevertheless, British rule was not unchallenged, as the Malayan Communist Party, the MCP, did cause problems.

In late 1951, Sir Henry Gurney, the British High Commissioner, was assassinated by the MCP. I remember reading about the assassination, as it was splashed over the pages of the local paper, The Straits Times. I remember, too, there was fear among the population during the Emergency years when the British Administration fought the communists, and Ah Heng whispering to MahMah about the murder of rubber estate managers by communists.

A new High Commissioner was sent out, Sir Gerald Templer, who became a hero. Through his tough measures he successfully defeated the MCP and their supporters. I recall the visit of Lady Templer to my school, run by English missionary Florence Carpenter and the Church of England. There were many English visitors. I clearly remember when pretty Princess Marina and the young Duke of Kent visited. We were at dancing class and we did an impromptu Scottish dance.

The English school I attended had Eurasian and Indian girls, but the majority were Chinese. There were only two Malay girls, sisters, in the senior classes. They were from a wealthy family and their father was a professional. In primary school I had a Gurkha friend. One year there were three Malay sisters, the first Malay girls I played with. Then they were gone!

It was only in Form 5 that I met a whole class of Malay students. This was in 1957, when my class was invited to a fun day with Form 5 at the Malay Girls College, an elite boarding school. By this time I had become outgoing and a class leader, as I spoke good English. That day I met the most beautiful, charming and accomplished Malay girls. The headmistress, an English lady who met us when we arrived, was the one responsible for our visit. The girls spoke good English and we got along well. We did folk dancing, at which they were even better than us, and had a guessing game or two. We were given lunch and an early tea. There was so much to eat. The girls were friendly and likeable. With further opportunities to meet I felt they would become my best friends! It was impossible not to enjoy ourselves. None wore a hijab. They were uninhibited and happy, full of laughter. These were days when English influence was strong. All girls wore shorts at games and at dancing sessions in the schools.

However, 1950 finds a listless Zhang family with two widows and many young children living in the family quarters on Batu Road. Zhang Yu had passed away less than a year before. Widow Foong Ying is deeply unhappy. Her good friend Hilda rings from Hong Kong, something she did not do when

Zhang Yu was alive. Knowing that MahMah enjoys opera, even if it is Cantonese and not Peking Opera, Hilda informs her that her friend, a young and talented actor, will be visiting Kuala Lumpur. Would Foong Ying like to meet and host him? MahMah consults Ah Heng, housekeeper and confidante. Ah Heng loves Cantonese opera and for the next two years the Shanghainese Zhang family become Cantonese opera fans.

MahMah has to do everything in style. She books two rows of the best seats every weekend. She sends the workers from the two shops to fill them. Then mid-week seats are booked. MahMah becomes the actor's godmother, and the godson is invited to stay at the shop. Soon the young actor's wife and toddler son join him. It is a good life for them: free food, accommodation and transport. After some months he and his family return to Hong Kong, for he still has a career to think of.

It is not the end of Cantonese opera for the Zhang family, for soon there is a replacement. An older "star" comes. He has appeared in a number of Hong Kong movies. He, too, takes up residence in the Zhang family quarters. Ah Heng is the happiest person: she loves the portrayals of heroes of the warring kingdoms from China's distant past. Most days she can be found preparing birds nest and chicken soup for the actors to preserve their singing voices. The actors eat well while Li and her siblings do not. Li is allowed to attend the shows, even the midweek operas, for she is an extra body to fill the seats. On some days at school it is a sleepy Li, for she has been at the opera. She still dreams of the fascinating sword dance from the night before, rather than focusing on what is on the blackboard.

1951 is also a sad year for Li. Ah Chieh had left the Zhang family. However, Li is lucky, for she had searched and found her. She sees Ah Chieh some three times a year, but it is not the same as living together. Once the novelty of the opera passes Li looks to school to fill her days.

Li learns to love school. She also finds that she can run, and is chosen to compete against girls two years older than she is.

But that competition sport is short-lived. as cooked breakfasts at home cease. Instead, she drinks a glass of warm water or eats a rusk or biscuit. Without sufficient breakfast to sustain her through the races, Li retches and vomits far too often to want to continue running. She is also small and not strongly built.

Li, indicated by the arrow, racing against the older girls

In 1952 Li is elated to find she has topped arithmetic in the mid-year exam. Unfortunately, there is no one at home to tell. Nobody is interested. She can get MahMah to sign her report card, which she does in Chinese, but she does not look at the subjects or question Li about her performance. Li decides that next time she will sign her own report card, for she can write her name in Chinese. The teachers will not know any better; it will be like Greek to them!

The Zhang children are educated in English while the adults were Chinese educated. Li knows she needs an identity card in Malaya, and persuades the shop manager, Cheong, to take her to the government department where they are issued. She gets a blue identity card, as she was born in Malaya, while her Indian classmates, who were born abroad, receive red ones.

In 1953 Li's father Jen and the rest of the family return from Singapore. Li continues life in the same way, same bed, same room in the top floor of the shop house. Her parents live on the floor below. They hardly come upstairs. They show no interest in Li and very little in Yeh. Jen has hit Li once, which hurt deeply, and she avoids him.

In 1954 Mei is starting to attract boys. Jen pronounces her the family beauty. Li wishes she looked like Mei. She loves watching Mei brush her long hair, which has a wave in it. Li often hears her parents' conversations in Shanghainese. They seem to enjoy talking about their children's abilities. Kwok, Mei and Sang are intelligent, Meng and Yeh are hardworking and Chien, although not intelligent, is the cute little beauty with her enormous eyes. She will have no difficulty finding a husband! Li does not rate a mention. She protests silently. Did they not know she was doing well in school and that she was popular?

Luk May, Meng, Mei, Li and Chien in 1955

Sister Mei takes Li along on her dates. Soon, Li finds she is being invited out herself. It gives her some joy that there are boys who find her interesting, even though her parents think little of her. And, in no time, Li finds herself in Form 5, a most interesting year.

Li aged 16

Li discovers that, because she enjoys literature, history and religious knowledge, she does well in them. Her artwork was so bad she had been allowed to drop the subject and now algebra and geometry were following the same pattern. Some of her classmates have private tuition, but it is expensive. Her parents would not pay for her so there is no point asking. However, 1957 was still a good year. Li is proud to be appointed a school prefect, honoured to wear the prefect's uniform and perform the duties that came with it.

The scene is the Victoria Institution and it is early 1958. Male and female students around 17 and 18 years of age laugh and chatter. There is giggling and smiles from the girls who come from different schools, and Li is there. She considers herself to be lucky, for she is standing among the elite. These are top students from the girls' schools in Kuala Lumpur, students way above her!

Li's social skills are still poor, yet she is two different persons. Li can turn on the sparkle and laugh, be charming, make friends and exude joy. She can draw people to herself.

Li feels her most confident this year.

Part 2 – The middle years

Li the Young Lady

In 1958 and 1959, Li is no longer a child but a young lady enjoying her two years in lower and upper sixth. Now going steady with Kit, she no longer dates anyone else. The exception is when her old boyfriend returns from abroad in 1960 and she keeps her promise to see him. They enjoy each other's company but decide to say goodbye and go their own way.

Twenty years later they bump into each other on the snowfields of Perisher Valley, Australia, with their respective partners. The four ski together for two days, then into the sunset to continue with their lives. They do not meet again.

Back to late 1958, Kit is now twenty-one years of age. KM finds that Kit has become serious about Li. KM and Grace decide to have a serious talk to him. Kit tells Li of the conversation afterwards. KM tells his son that marriage is a serious matter, and one does not choose a lifetime partner because a girl has a sweet smile. Grace adds that pretty girls are plentiful. That all Chinese families have certain requirements. The girl must be from a good background and a virgin. Her educational background and the family's financial standing are important. Are there siblings? And lastly the mother. Having many children means she was fertile, a trait she likely passed on to her daughters. Kit, as an only son, has a duty to continue the family line.

As time passes KM takes to Li. He likes her honesty and they enjoyed chatting together.

KM learns much about Li's family. Although her father has no fondness for Li, he is still very traditional. He is unlikely to allow an outsider to finance his daughter's education, for he would lose face. By the end of 1959 KM feels that Li is worth educating and he would like her for a daughter.

Before the university year starts in 1960, Kit and Li are engaged. Father Jen is happy as he does not lose face, even though someone else is financing Li's studies. His daughter is almost married, as she is betrothed. She has left the Zhang family as far as he is concerned.

Kit's father makes the decisions from now on. KM decides that Li should study in the university of Singapore rather than the newly opened university in Kuala Lumpur, so the young couple will be together. Li sees Grace and KM only during the vacation. With KM in control all goes well.

In her second year. Li asks Kit's permission to join the Students' Union Council. A few years earlier Kit had been on the council. She stands for election and becomes the representative for the ladies' residential college. She is no firebrand, having reverted to her earlier shyness, and does not have the confidence to speak. She would like to contribute but decides to stay quiet for fear of making a fool of herself. Li does what is expected of her on the social committee, helping to entertain guests and help organise social functions. She finishes her year, happy to have served and to have learnt how the student council functions.

In early 1962, Li is 21 and Kit is 24. Both are in their final year. They have been going steady for four years, engaged for two. They begin to think of marriage. Li wants a small private wedding, better still if they could elope. Kit knows his parents would be hurt if they did that. His mother had never stopped complaining about the small engagement ring Li wore, because Li had refused to borrow money from her or allow Grace to help her choose a 'decent size diamond.' Grace could not fathom Li – surely all females love diamonds! Kit knew Grace wanted a big wedding for her only son. Kit and Li had heard Grace talking about a big wedding. It was to be Grace's special night, for she was to be decked out in her finery, in a long cheongsam and long white gloves, meeting and greeting the numerous guests at the entrance of the Federal Hotel, which had the largest and best decorated restaurant in Kuala Lumpur.

Again, Grace's plans are sabotaged by Li. Kit talks his father into a small wedding luncheon for relatives and very close family friends.

Perhaps it was at this point of time that Grace decides that Li must be remade.

Kit had not dropped her as she had hoped. Li cannot be allowed to do as she pleased. Why couldn't Li be obedient and do as she was told. But Grace would have to be careful, for her husband liked Li. Would he allow her to remake Li?

Grace had been careful not to make known to her husband her true feelings about Li. Grace had not taken to Kit's former girlfriend either, or, for that matter, to any of his girlfriends. The previous one, a pretty girl, was the first of many sisters and her family was not affluent. What if Kit had to support all the younger siblings? All Li had was a sweet smile, maybe her bright eyes as well. But all of them could not be compared to herself, Grace felt. There were so many things wrong with Li. To start with, she came from those weird Shanghainese. Grace had only heard of them and their queer habits. Grace and KM were locally born and English educated. Grace was born to a devout Methodist mother. Li came from a Buddhist family. She was a little heathen.

In fact, the Zhang family were not devout Buddhists, but neither were they without values. The teachings of sage Confucius were taught to the children. They were taught to be honest, truthful and respectful. The girls were sent to an Anglican missionary school, where they were taught Christian principles. Every day there was morning assembly, which started and ended with the singing of hymns that Li loved. It was followed by religious knowledge lessons in class. When Grace thought of reforming her, Li had already discovered western philosophy. Li enjoyed the works of John Stuart Mill and his writings on Unitarianism.

A Glimpse Into Early Married Life

Kit and me: A rented room

What was our life like? A look into our lives.

In May 1962, with father-in-law KM's encouragement, we moved into a room in sister-in-law Chun's house. It was a large wooden bungalow, official quarters, as Chun's husband, Chuan, worked as a doctor for the Singapore government. Kit was in his final year of medicine and I in my final year of Arts. I was expecting our first child. We owned a Mini Minor, and Kit drove me to university every morning for lectures and picked me up in the late afternoon.

It was good of Chun to offer us the room. My father-in-law was most happy, as Chun, also a doctor, would keep an eye on my health. This was the first child bearing his surname, hopefully a male. For Chun, the money that had gone to my hostel fees now went to her. Her husband did not want her to work, but he still had to help with his brothers with their education fees, and poor Chun had a hard time juggling the household expenses. By now she had two boys, a three year old and the younger one, who was a few months old.

I was on my best behaviour and did not voice my opinions. Both Chun and Chuan had very strong opinions. What was the point of offending them? Besides they were kind and helpful.

The household was run most parsimoniously. Chuan had little idea of expenses and Chun had little choice, but never complained. She was besotted by her husband and had agreed to a big family with many sons! He was a simple, happy person and they were a compatible couple, very much in love.

Chun employed a professional black and white amah after her first son came along. Following the birth of number two, the amah, Ah Kwan, agreed to stay on and help look after the boys as Chun breastfed. Chun gave Ah Kwan medical attention for her minor ailments and Ah Kwan agreed to do simple cooking. Kit and I ate lunch at the University canteen, barely any breakfast (a piece of bread and butter is all we were given) and dinner at home. The meals were healthy but bland. No salt or spices were allowed by Chuan, as he considered them harmful. Every dinner was the same frugal fare.

Right from the beginning Chun had declared that they were no gourmands and food was a low priority. Chuan laughingly stated that he ate to live and why waste money when everything 'goes down the gutter!'

Come October of the same year we moved out of Chun's house to a rented room in an old house some distance from the city, as rent was cheap there. On our first day in the new place, and in control of our money again, we went to the Balestier Road food stalls, dined on clay pot chicken rice and a big bowl of chicken mushroom soup. The food was delicious and we enjoyed it so much!

Both Kit and I were free spirits. We could not stay caged. And we loved our food!

We returned, contented, to our rented room, which, though old, was spacious. It had an old rickety bed, a large old desk and two chairs. Everything was old except us!

As we sat down on the chairs our eyes met. We both grinned. A peal of laughter escaped from me and Kit joined in. We read each other's thoughts.

'We escaped!'

No more Tuesday nights when I had to look after Chun's second boy, who was often crying and throwing up. No more lectures on religion and how to lead a good life from Chuan. Kit would run off, saying he was meeting up with his study group. I was desperately short of study time, yet could not tell them that the Philosophy department required me to answer why I should not be barred from the forthcoming exams, having attended less than 50% of the lectures. It was a subject I enjoyed so much, but my morning sickness had been bad, and

I was throwing up often, how could I attend lectures? In my history class I was so sick I had to put my head down on the desk. At the next lecture the professor said he did not want to see anyone sleeping in his class. It was directed at me. I never expected such a remark from a mature Englishman, but then, I had no baby bump till the fifth month, when I bloated and started to waddle like a duck!

I think my relief might have been the greater, but Kit was laughing more than me and we could not stop. 'Hold it,' I said. 'I have a stitch on my side.' Kit looked at his over-seven months pregnant wife. 'I do not want you to go into premature labour.' The sudden serious look on his face started me laughing again.

Yes, Kit and I used to laugh a lot. It used to annoy Grace and she told me – not Kit – to quieten down. Often it was Kit who started it. We shared a sense of humour. It helped keep us together. We were married for almost 58 years.

Yeh, Li and the Crown Prince of Brunei

I seemed to lead a charmed life, for I got to meet so many prominent people. It was at the Victoria Institution in 1963 that I met the young Crown Prince of Brunei, who was a student in Form 3. I was the replacement teacher for Mrs Tan, who was on maternity leave. (I had already done a short stint of teaching practice there when I did my diploma in education).

Hassanal Bolkiah was a serious, good looking boy. He was well built and towered above his classmates. He was the class monitor and took his duties seriously. One duty was to attend to the cleaning of the blackboard. Every classroom had a large blackboard hanging on the wall at the front. Mathematics and science teachers would often fill up every part of the board and the monitor had to clear it before the next lesson. I covered history and English and used the board less. It was also the monitor's duty to collect the books from the students if there was work to be handed in. The monitor would bring them to the teacher's desk in the staff room, and this he did for me. I found him pleasant and respectful.

The Crown Prince of Brunei, aged 15, at the Victoria Institute

It was my brother Yeh who had the more "exciting" encounter. Yeh was the chemistry teacher, and apparently the only person to touch the royal forehead!

This is the scene described to me. Yeh was walking between the rows of seated students and teaching at the same time. Some teachers do not stay on one spot. He stopped suddenly and directed a question to the nearest student while still looking downwards. He did not get the answer he wanted so he raised two fingers to give a friendly rap to the boy's head. (These were the days when teachers could do that and caning was allowed.) When Yeh looked up, whose head had he touched? Of the whole class of boys, Hassanal Bolkiah was the last person he expected. The bodyguard stationed at the back of the class rushed forward. The young prince waved him back. Perhaps this was an indication of a good ruler-to-be, not an arrogant or vengeful person.

The bad mother

During the years from 1964 to early 1966 Li and Kit were in rural Malaysia, as Kit was serving out his scholarship. They are now back in KL. In 1966 they welcome a daughter. In 1967 they are settled, and it was time, Grace seems to feel, to work on Li and make her a better person.

Li, like most in the Zhang family, has a siesta in the afternoon. Perhaps the habit grew when the family was acclimatising from cold Shanghai to the Malayan climate, as the heat made them sleepy. Except, Zhang Yu, who never succumbed to the habit. He was just too busy. Kit's family did not have such a practice.

Grace enlists Chun's support. Li is surprised by a sudden visit from Chun, only learning later that it was at Grace's request. Chun has noticed that Li has regular siestas after the children come home from school. Mother and daughter confront Li one afternoon after her siesta. 'You are a bad mother. You do not do enough for your children. You should sacrifice the siesta time for your children.' Grace adds 'You should be playing with them or teaching them. It is for your own good to bond with the children.'

Li returns quietly to her room. She does not argue or remonstrate. She is in pain. Kit's sister and mother have both condemned her. They believe that she is selfish, indulgent, more concerned with self-interest, full of tricks and play-acting, as they think that was how she had gained KM's sympathy.

Li prays. 'I am not a liar and an unworthy person. I am so tired after working a day in school, I just cannot keep my eyes opened. Besides, how do I keep myself fresh for Kit? He is so full of energy. He wants to go to a show or eat out with friends. And I have my devoted Ah Yoke to help look after the kids.

'Chun, please do not strip me of the last of my self-belief', Li pleads inwardly. She visits "dark places" again.

1970 Travels

I described our first time in Australia in *The Reluctant Migrant's Daughter*. On our return to Malaysia in 1969 we found that the country, with its multi racial population, was not as harmonious as when we left for Australia in late 1967. The May 13th riots were a shock and we could have lost our lives. Kit was still hopeful. He was sure things would improve. In August I found a new job as a librarian and was most happy to be working, as Kit and I had no savings. Besides, faithful Ah Yoke was still with me. The one regret was perhaps re-employing Ah Mui, Grace's old cook and housekeeper. Her loyalties laid with Grace. Ah Mui helped create a toxic atmosphere with her daily reports when Grace came for dinner each night. Her usefulness extended to showing Grace all my newly purchased items, whether household or personal things, whenever Kit and I were out for a social evening.

I started to enjoy my new job. It became even more interesting when I learnt there was the possibility of a study trip to London through the British Council. But first I needed to talk to Kit. Would he be agreeable to me going to London for three months? Ah Yoke and Ah Mui were reliable workers. Grace lived two kilometres away and Kit, working at the University hospital and lecturing, had fewer night duties. He was still passionate about his golf. As long as there was still daylight Kit would be chasing the little white ball. The kids and his love affair with golf would help keep him busy. The ever-cheerful Kit felt that I should not miss out if the chance of a study trip came along. And the chance did come along. My visits to the British Council paid off. My employers agreed to paid leave. Everything else was my own responsibility: airfare, accommodation, food. I was off to London to learn about news librarianship at Reuters.

I arranged to stay with a university classmate who was working for the Singapore Government. Shopping around for cheap airfares, I found the best from Aeroflot, the Russian airline. An additional attraction was the overnight stay in Moscow and a morning tour, all free!

It was on a morning in April that I stepped off the plane, hugging my thick coat. It was sister Mei's coat, one she used for the two years she lived in England. It was a surprise to find Moscow so warm! I'd seen the film Dr Zhivago just months earlier and expected it to be cold. At the airport I was met by an airline official and told that my overnight accommodation was within walking distance and that a guide and car would be there for me the next morning to tour Moscow.

I rested a few hours in the small hostel room, for the flight had been exhausting. Then, while there was still light, I took a slow walk back to the airport. I was hungry now, having only eaten half the sandwich I was given for dinner on the flight.

But first the airport shops. I wanted to buy a Dr Zhivago hat for Kit. There were plenty of them in the shops, but the prices were just too much. Almost half a month's salary! Kit would have to do without. I bought a comparatively cheap scarf for myself. One full of hammers and sickles, which still hangs in my cupboard today.

For dinner I found a soup that tasted of salt water and a slice of black bread, of which I managed only two bites, but reminded myself that I did not come for the food but the sights. I was asked to pay in US dollars. By this time the moon had come out. In the moonlight I walked back to my room in the hostel. The song 'Somewhere my love', Laura's Theme from Dr Zhivago, superimposed itself onto my brain as I dreamily walked along. Whenever I hear the tune I recall that night in Moscow. Only Kit was missing!

Back in the room, the door had no lock so I placed the only chair against it. Maybe the noise would warn me if someone did try to break in. A pleasant looking lady and a car appeared the next day, so we sped off to Red Square.

Red Square was exactly as depicted in the postcards. There was the iconic St Basil's Cathedral, the Grand Kremlin Palace and the Moskva River. Lenin's Mausoleum was closed for repairs, so no visits were possible. Then it was back to the airport and onwards to London.

I was fortunate to stay at Golders Green, a beautiful part of London. My classmate, Lian, lived in a lovely cottage there. Lian was a most gracious host. It was she who told me that an acquaintance had a ticket to sell for the tulip tour in The Netherlands. Lian told me that the tulip tours were often booked out and I should not miss the opportunity. I grabbed it and turned up for work four days late!

The tulip tour was good value, as promised. The day at the Keukenhof Garden was unforgettable. It was the tulip season at its best and what I saw was the most beautiful scene in my life. Tulips, tulips everywhere, as far as eye could see, fields and fields of tulips. All the glorious shades of red, pink and purple, in-between shades, as well as black tulips. It left me breathless, lifted my spirit and filled me with joy! I recalled the words of William Wordsworth's *I wandered lonely as a cloud* when he was carried away by the beauty of "a host, of golden daffodils". Wordsworth committed the scene to memory when he wrote "I gazed – and gazed – but little thought, What wealth the show to me had brought…"

I recall another scene that left me breathless, this time with awe. It was sixteen years later in 1986 when I stood dumbstruck as I looked at the rows of entombed warriors in Xian, China. I was proud to be Chinese, to belong to such a great civilisation.

While drinking in the beauty of the tulips I felt that I must bring Kit here one day. But it never happened, as he was not interested. It was golf and skiing that interested him.

During the study trip I took the opportunity to see Paris. It was only an hour away by air. I saw the Eiffel Tower and the Champs-Élysées. I was to see more of these two places when, years later, Kit and I visited Paris during a side trip on our "Ski France" holiday.

Back to London. It was time to come home. I do not think I could stomach another flight on an Aeroflot plane. Once in a lifetime was enough! The flight had left Kuala Lumpur with two passengers. I was so miserably cold I thought I would have frozen if not for Mei's thick coat. At Karachi a few more passengers came on board, but it was still too cold.

If I returned by Scandinavia Airlines I could stay overnight at Copenhagen. I remembered the song *Wonderful Copenhagen*, which was one of the most cheerful songs I have come across. After being told that I would get a refund from Aeroflot (I was misinformed), I proceeded to purchase a ticket from SAS to fly to wonderful Copenhagen.

I visited the famous Tivoli Gardens in the evening of my arrival. Ella Fitzgerald, the Queen of Jazz, was in concert. I wasn't particularly a fan, but I was lucky to get a ticket. She gave her usual high standard performance. I went backstage and found a crowd there. Her manager said she was tired and wanted no more than ten fans. Being the only Asian in the crowd I was selected. Ella spent a few minutes with me. She wanted to know where I was from and my nationality. She was kind and gracious. Then she signed her autograph on a piece of paper. I brought that with me when I migrated to Australia, but must have lost it during one of my many moves.

The next morning I went to see the bronze statue of The Little Mermaid by the waterside at Langelinie. I took the river cruise as well. Then it was back to my loved ones. I wanted to go home.

An encounter with Muhammad Ali

A highlight while living in Ipoh was the 200 km trip to Kuala Lumpur for the World Heavyweight Championship title fight. It was Muhammad Ali against Joe Bugner at the Merdeka stadium on 30 June 1975.

When news of the forthcoming fight reached Kit he could hardly believe it. What, in an Asian country? He told good friend and colleague Andrew, and they planned to skip work and make the four hour round trip to watch it. Kit booked the tickets.

The day was approaching, but where was Andrew? Andrew was still on holiday overseas with his wife! Soon it was clear that the expensive ticket was to go begging. Kit would have to give it away. Li approached Kit. She did not like to watch people being beaten up at any time, but this was a once in a lifetime event, a sport, and Li loved running down to her home town.

Kit and Li had good seats, but they would still be watching from a short distance away. Li was in for a pleasant surprise.

Come the day and Kit and Li found their seats. They were early, the crowd was growing and the excitement mounting. Li thought it would be prudent to make a visit to the ladies' room. She headed for the far end of the stadium, then she was lost. She always had a poor sense of direction. No one was around. Strange, she must have taken a wrong turn. But wait, there was a group of people approaching.

An entourage of some seven persons walked towards her. As they came nearer the one near the middle stood out. This tall guy with rippling muscles was a prime specimen of manhood! They were almost face to face. It was Muhammad Ali!

Li stood transfixed. She thought of running away but could not move. A woolly-haired guy with a leer called out 'Hello baby.' 'Yuk', thought Li, only having eyes for that outstanding masculine figure. Muhammed Ali gave a gentle smile and a wink and then he was gone. They were heading for the boxing ring. Could Li ever forget the kind look on his face? She had met Muhammad Ali!

Grace, Jewellery and Mind Games

Friends are amazed that Grace can trouble Li when they live in separate places with an ocean in between! How?

In the early 1980s Grace starts coming to Sydney regularly. On one occasion she brings her partner, San. San is treated with courtesy and respect. This is Kit's house, and his relatives are welcomed.

One year Grace brings a gift of jewellery. Grace loves jewellery and wears earrings and lockets all the time. Li has little time or money for jewellery, although by this time she can afford to buy bits and pieces if she is so inclined. She is not.

Over the years Grace has built up a collection of moderately priced jade and gold items bought from the pawnshops where many a Chinese housewife had to sell jewellery to buy food during the years of Japanese occupation.

Grace hands Li a small but pretty diamond locket and chain. A good buy for a modest Malaysian $1,300 (AU $400). There is always a receipt from the goldsmiths. Goldsmith shops were common and popular in Chinatown. With the receipt one could redeem the original price, less 10%, for cash. (Once I had mentioned to Grace that I was unable to give my mother a decent ang pow for her trip to China, as I would not get my pay cheque until the end of the month. Presents to my side of the family came from my pay. Grace reminded me that I had a gold bracelet, a combined wedding present from Kit's aunts, which I could redeem at the goldsmiths. It was at her suggestion and with her permission I handed the bracelet and receipt to Luk May. Luk May always returned something. She bought a pram for my daughter on her way through Hong Kong.)

Li is wary of Grace and not keen to accept her present. Grace is insistent and Kit is pleased with his mother's present. Grace says she knows I have little in the way of jewellery and this is presentable for wearing to functions with Kit's colleagues. In the privacy of our bedroom Kit reminds me that, although the gift could not be considered expensive, it had still cost Grace money and Grace was always so careful with money!

For so many weeks after Li is in emotional turmoil. Kit again mentions that his mother is a kindly woman. At night in bed Li cannot sleep. She berates herself, calling herself names for being so hard on his mother! But what about the hatred |Grace has shown and the things she has said. Was the gift a peace offering? Why doesn't Li forget the past and start anew? But Grace has condemned Li and cost her so much pain.

An over-sensitive daughter-in-law who fails to handle/manage a slightly insensitive mother-in-law. That was Kit's conclusion.

Grace is back the next year. Again, Li is thrown into emotional turmoil. The afternoon after her arrival, when Kit is at work, Grace enters Li bedroom. Li asks if she needs something. Grace wants to know where the diamond necklace is, since Li is not wearing it. Li tells her it is in the little safe just across from the bed, as she only wears it at functions. Li cannot believe Grace's next sentence: 'Since you do not wear it, can I have it back?' Unsure whether Grace sees the tears coming to her eyes, Li replies that she will get it straightaway. She goes to the safe, turns the combination and brings out the little jewellery box. Li hands over the box and Grace makes a quick exit.

Li is in for another surprise. As Grace makes her way to her granddaughter's room, the next one after the bathroom, her voice rings out. 'Granddaughter, I have a present for you, a diamond locket I brought from Malaysia.'

Li bites her lips as she controls her emotions. 'Indian giver, Indian giver, why do I allow you to play havoc with my emotions', she thinks … Ten years later it happened again with jade earrings. A fool never learns.

The jade earrings

Grace had hinted time and again, if Li would be obedient and did as Grace wanted, Li could find herself rewarded with pieces of jewellery from the collection Grace had built up over the years. To Grace, all women loved jewellery and did not understand why there was no response from Li. If only Grace realised that Li would never sell her independence.

In 1977, when Kit, Li and their children were leaving Malaysia, Grace called Li aside and handed her two items of jewellery. Li was surprised. There was a pretty jade brooch, but more interesting was a pair of jade earrings. They were dangling earrings with a simple hook, but could look good if reset by a jeweller. Grace had a more expensive pair, so this was the poor cousin. Li was puzzled at being handed the items. 'That is your share of the jewellery', Grace said.

Li wearing the jade earrings

Maybe Grace decided that Li should have the two items by virtue of being Kit's wife. Li took a liking to the jade earrings. She thought they look good and matched the cheongsam that

Chun gave her. Li was happy with the earrings and wore them at the wedding of her second son in 1993.

Grace did not visit for the first few years after her son's migration to Sydney. Li heard she had been busy travelling with partner San. Then she was in Sydney with San. Sadly, the hostility was back again.

Grace began visiting every second year and then every year. One morning in 1995 Grace asked Li about the two jade items she had given her, and if Li was no longer wearing them could she please return them? Li could not believe her ears and walked away. Two days later Grace asked again for them. Li agonised. What should she do? Li did not care about the brooch but the earrings had become part of her. Could she offer to buy the earrings from Grace? They were not even really expensive items. Could she refuse to return them? They were Grace's originally, and now she wanted them back. Li decided that she had no right to cling on to them. She'd had them for almost 20 years and handed them back to Grace. That night, while Grace slept her good sleep in the guest room – as she said, she has no difficulty sleeping anytime – and Kit slept the sleep of an exhausted worker, Li wept in her bed, for she had to said goodbye to something she had really liked.

When Grace passed away Li asked Kit to approach Chun for the jade earrings. That was the only item she wanted, and it had been hers for so many years. Chun had always tried to be fair and searched for them, but they were nowhere to be found. Chun said they were probably given away.

Perhaps Li had handled things wrongly again. Li had felt she had been true to herself. She could not be a hypocrite, nor could she pretend. Was her pain self-inflicted?

Li would love to know where the jade earrings are.

Know thyself: A last meeting with Grace

It is 2009, my last meeting with Grace. Kit and I are at the nursing home in Singapore. We visit every year, as Grace is increasingly frail. This year she is 92. In fact, I am back because my own mother, Luk May, passed away a week before in Kuala Lumpur. I have come to pay my last respects and scatter her ashes with my siblings. But first we stop in Singapore to see Grace, as she is unwell.

We are in Grace's room. Kit sits on the seat to her left while I am on her right. Grace is tossing on her bed. She no longer walks. Chun tells us that Grace does not always recognise her.

I see this person with straight white hair and a frail body lying on the bed before me. What are my thoughts? All I want is to catch her attention when she opens her eyes. They flutter and she opens her eyes. I called out 'Mum, Kit is here, he is sitting just near you.' Kit lifts his head to look at her and smiles at Grace. She looks at him. Signs of recognition appear and she fixes her eyes on him. Their eyes linger on each other. The love is there.

This is wonderful. I know that Kit wants Grace to know he loves her and for this message to reach her one last time. It gives me joy to recall this scene because it tells me what I am. The scene cleanses my soul. I learn of myself. The person Li can be proud of, for I allowed love to dominate.

I know I had no hatred or selfishness on that day, no thought of myself. My love for Kit made me want him to have that moment of love with his mother. I am true to little Li. All I wanted was for mother and son to share their love for perhaps the last time.

In writing this second volume of memoirs I have gained even more insights into myself. I have no need to be ashamed of myself, and have no need to apologise. Little Li has grown up, she is no longer the child of little value, but a person of integrity and love, at peace with herself. It has taken a long time, but in 2023 it is a proud Li who is at the end of her journey.

Part 3 – The later years

Happy Days of Travel

It was not until the 1990s that we felt free to travel. The children had finished their studies, we had paid off our home mortgage and now had funds to travel. No, not money to burn, but Kit and I were never extravagant. After all, we lived well enough.

Cruising

During one of our frugal ski holidays we discovered how relaxing a sea cruise could be, taking a three day cruise along the western coast of the USA.

Cruising presented an entire new world. Breakfast and lunch were buffet-style, dinner was seated and served. There was a good selection of food, as much as you wanted. On deck there were swimming pools and lounge chairs for sunbathing or a snooze. We preferred a walk and the sea breeze. Within the ship there was the gym, the bar and live music.

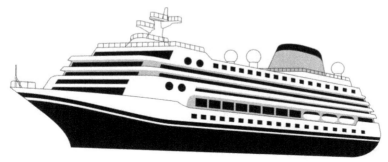

In 2002 we went on our first big cruise to Alaska, seeing a part of the world we had not known and animals with which we were unfamiliar. Cruises were now part of our holiday itinerary, first on the Holland American Line, then the Cunard Line. Cunard had bigger ships with more to offer.

Cunard offered the indulgence of a dance band every night. Kit and I both loved to dance and were always the last pair left on the floor. I had observed the Malay joget girls at the Sultan of Pahang's parties and learnt to move my shoulders and body. Along with the young crowd, I could never resist Neil Diamond's *Sweet Caroline*. And wasn't I pleased when stopped by a lady in her thirties and complimented on my dancing! To my delight, she said she had watched me the night before, adding that I was the best dancer by far!

The cruises had so much to offer. Kit learnt to appreciate the fine wine that came with the good food. The good dining was followed by high quality shows performed by dance troupes and singers. Yet the night was not over, for there was still the casino. Kit would play Blackjack, while I went for the poker machines. While I had lousy luck and poor control, Kit had good gambling skills and good control. He always covered my losses.

Touring

Touring has its own magic, visiting places of which one has previously only dreamed. The difference for me was being on solid ground, a change from the lazy cruise where one is pampered with food and drinks all day or the exhausting day in the snow, trudging back to the lodge in heavy boots with heavier skis on your shoulders. Nor the worry when you have missed a turn and find yourself alone on a black snow run. How to get out alive? But then again, it is a different story when you are gliding on the soft smooth snow. Can anything else be as exhilarating?

Ha! I have worked out a cheap and interesting holiday. We can add three or four days to our week's visit to Grace in Kuala Lumpur. Kit had found Egypt fascinating. I had worked in a stopover there on our way to ski in Switzerland. Since then he had found good stopovers acceptable. I am able to persuade Kit to do a short trip in Jogjakarta, Indonesia.

Borobudur

Borobudur is where I want to visit. I wish to see as many historical sites as I can. Of course, I did not tell Kit that Borobudur might be boring.

Borobudur is 40 kilometres from Jogjakarta. It is the largest Buddhist temple in the world, an eighth century Mahayana Buddhist temple with 2,672 relief panels and 504 Buddhist statues. It was abandoned in the 14th century and hidden for centuries under layers of volcanic ash and jungle growth. It is an enigma, for there is little information on this place, but Borobudur has been listed as a World Heritage Site since 1991.

Borobudur

Here we are, standing in the midst of Buddhist stupas and statues. I run my fingers over the statues, as it must have been touched centuries before. There are few tourists around and the place is rather quiet. Yet this was a thriving centre in its heyday. During its long period of construction there must have been thousands of workers, homes for the labourers, kitchens to feed them. People who lived. People who knew joy and sorrow like us.

Were families allowed? Are there no answers still? Perhaps one day soon. I look forward to the next day, for we are to visit the palace of Hamengkubuwono IX, the previous sultan of Jogjakarta. His palace is opened to tourists.

The vast sitting room is full of photographs. I am delighted. There are photos of the Sultan with Soekarno and with other freedom fighters. They had fought the Dutch, the colonial masters, who would not return the country to its people, for it brought them so much wealth. It was the colony that was described as 'the cork that kept the Netherlands afloat.' My interest in history made me appreciate the freedom fighters who fought for the love of their country. They cannot lose, they will never lose! This proved to be true with the Vietnam War years later.

Bali

The next year we visit Bali, Australia's favourite holiday island. It is cheap and close. The morning after arrival we are there but so is everyone else! The beach is a thriving business centre. There are bodies lying everywhere, sunbathers and those enjoying a massage. Teenage girls are having their hair twisted into a dozen or more plaits, the current popular style. Local youths hawk their wares. Half a dozen of them are selling cheap colourful watches. We are not the "sun and surf" type, but we are interested in seeing the country. We hire a car and driver and head for the mountains.

Our driver is in his thirties, pleasant and friendly. Kit speaks good Malay, and since it is similar to Indonesian they are chatting away. I will tell you why he is interesting! Kit is seated in the front passenger seat and I sit at the back, observing the driver. Every few minutes he plunges the long fingernail on his right little finger into his mop of dark hair and has a good scratch. I work out his problem. He has nits. It is a common problem among the poor in the remote villages in Malaysia.

I remember the day before when I had been in the shopping centre. There were a number of small galleries. We had seen paintings of young Balinese ladies, lying on the laps of older ladies. They were having the nits picked out of their hair. Kit had asked me if we should buy one of them to hang in the sitting room. It would be a good subject for conversation. I gave him a scornful look reinforced by 'Yuk!' Actually, the paintings were quite well done.

We had a good time going up the mountains that day. We passed small villages with their attap leaf roofs along the road. Some of the houses were no bigger than a large room. Each time as we neared a village there would be a stall or two selling little shrivelled up papayas or mangoes, with the odd durian hanging above them. The stalls were often attended by an old lady or a young girl. We stopped for a drink at a hotel on the way. It was a bottled drink, as Kit wanted no food poisoning in a country that had sanitation problems.

A short distance later I saw a small stall that had souvenirs for sale. I wanted little gifts to bring home. A blouse that was hung up high caught my eye. The stall was tended by a girl of about fifteen years of age. She had to bring a ladder from the back to climb up to get to the hanging blouse. I smiled at her for bringing it down. Yes, I liked it. I wanted to check that the size was right, only to find it was ripped down the side. I could see that it was more than a simple repair job. The girl offered to give me a discount. But how could I buy a torn garment? I was thinking of giving her some money as she looked distressed. At that point our driver ushered me out of the shop as he felt he had to protect his customer, me. He had seen the damaged blouse. We drove off, but I felt I should have given the girl a couple of dollars. Probably there had been no sales for the day. I asked the driver to stop by on the way back so I could compensate her. We visited the golf course on the way up and then an extinct volcano. We stopped at the scenic points, enjoying the cool mountain air and its quiet beauty. By the time we came down the mountains it was sunset, the driver had forgotten about the girl, and it was too far to go back when I remembered to ask about her.

The next day we saw two Balinese dances. The first was the traditional Balinese dance performed by young girls. This classical dance is slow, and the movements are concentrated in the fingers, eyes and head. The dancers move as one. These young girls have trained for a long time. It is very graceful, a far cry from the fast dances of teenagers now. But I also appreciate the energetic dances of our modern times!

Balinese dance

We are driven to another place where we are treated to a different dance. We watched the Barong, a mythical animal in Indonesian folklore, which protects humans. The dancers wear animal costumes. The movements are fast, full of leaps and bounds. A little like the Chinese acrobatic movements. It is entertaining and the audience applauds.

The next day is our last in Bali and we are taken to the temple. Unlike the rest of Indonesia, which is Muslim, Bali is Hindu. We see the Balinese women move around gracefully with baskets of fruits balanced on their heads. That evening we are entertained by a gamelan music concert of percussion instruments. Kit has been looking forward to it. The sounds from the percussion instruments are soothing, pleasing to the ear. It leaves one with a feeling of peace. It is a fitting end to our week in Bali.

South America

In July 2000 Kit and I visit South America. The trip, as with all our trips, is the result of my scheming and planning. The trip is expensive and includes three countries: Argentina, Brazil and Peru. I could not think of a more exciting adventure!

Argentina

The day arrives. We fly on the long, exhausting trip to Buenos Aires.

The next morning we are taken to tour the city sights. That evening we go to a dinner and show. Of course, the show is a tango performance with the full band. Kit and I sit transfixed, for we loved the tango – allegedly banned in 1914 by the Pope for being immoral – since we were teenagers but could find no one to teach us at the time. It was in Sydney that we learnt it. By then I had two bad knees, could not move fast enough and was not young. Kit fared much better. He had the tango "pose" and he moved well.

We are taken to Caminito, the place where the dance began. As we look around the city we find the dance being performed on the streets. Couples no longer in their prime, but still splendid dancers, give demonstrations. It is good even with the taped music. We leave some money in the hat for what we had enjoyed. Another evening we are taken to a dance studio where novices are doing the dance. Even they are good. We are so bold as to take to the floor. Kit is good, but I feel I am too slow, as my left foot with the ACL damage sometimes plays up.

We pay for a last good show. It is not just the dancers, but a quality band that brings out the magic of the tango.

The treats continue. The Iguazu Falls – Cataratas del Iguazu – is awesome, plunging into a massive gorge. A total of 275 falls along a three kilometre front, with an average height of 70 metres. How can it not impress? From our hotel, the Sheraton International, one of the most expensive of the tour, we are able to see part of the Falls and hear the roar. From the viewing platform and in cheap rain coats we still got drenched!

Brazil

On Day 5 we take a flight to Rio de Janeiro, Brazil, arriving when it is dark. We are taken to our hotel on Copacabana beach. As the night is still young Kit fancies a walk. We talk to hotel reception, inquiring about the beach just across the road. The receptionist turns pale. It is the easiest way to get mugged. You may even get stabbed. Please take your walk in bright daylight. I tell Kit I will not let him go. I definitely have no plans to become a widow at this stage!

Next morning we visit the statue of Christ the Redeemer. It is a cloudy day, but the clouds clear for a few moments while I take a photo in front of the statue. Kit has no such luck.

We move on to Sugar Loaf Mountain, taking the cable car to the top of the mountain to enjoy the superb city views.

On Day 7 we visit the markets. There an old lady tries to sell me a packet consisting of a small dead bird, a few dried flowers and leaves, some earth, and odd bits I have no wish to identify. It is supposed to be a powerful charm but I want nothing to do with it! In the market I see the Brazilian poor, dark skinned individuals, others light brown, yet others fair. They resemble their indigenous ancestors, or those from Africa, Portugal, or have inherited a mixture of genes from the conquerors, imported slaves and the locals. The country is of interest to us because one of our sons married a Brazilian girl.

Peru

Finally, we are ready to visit Peru. The history buff will get her enjoyment, for she will get to see Machu Picchu.

We fly into Lima. It is late and we are tired from the travelling and waiting at airports.

The next day we get to see the city. Peru's Spanish heritage is visible in the cathedrals, promenades and old buildings. Lima sits on the Pacific coast and was the centre of Spanish trade. An English-speaking guide takes us around. This South American trip is not an organised tour, so it is just us and the guide. We walk to a corner of the cathedral where there is a large grill on the floor through which rises a fishy smell. The guide tells us there is a dungeon below containing thousands of bones of tortured prisoners who died during the Spanish Inquisition. On many a night, when the breeze blows, the screams of those tortured can be heard, he says!

That night Kit and I each have a steak at a restaurant with a small pan pipe band. They play the Simon and Garfunkel tune *El Condor Pasa (If I Could)*. I enjoy hearing the pan pipes. They invoke a sad nostalgia. I get to see a llama, but am not pleased when told that what I ate was llama steak.

On the next day we fly over the Andes to the old Inca capital of Cusco.

Cusco is 3,310 m above sea level in the high Peruvian Andes. It has extensive Inca ruins as well colonial churches, monasteries and convents. For a change we arrive in bright daylight and are taken straight to the hotel to rest and acclimatise. I feel slightly sick. Kit feels fine, so he walks off to familiarise himself with the place. Ha, fifteen minutes later he is back; the altitude has started to affect him. The next day we explore Cusco. Finally, on the third day we go to the railway station for the trip to Machu Picchu.

Machu Picchu, Lost City of the Incas, an important ceremonial centre of the Incas where human sacrifices were made. It was overgrown by tropical vegetation for centuries until Hiram Bingham, an American historian, was guided to it by locals in 1911. I read about it so many years ago. What a charming romantic story. Now I am going to see it. The zigzag train ride with the train shunting to and fro is tedious, but we get there.

The scene from the top of the ruins is delightful. It is like a picture book, but I am not overwhelmed. We wander through the ruins. It would have helped my appreciation and imagination if there was more information about the place.

Li at Machu Picchu

We retire to the only hotel up there, Machu Picchu Sanctuary Lodge. We are lucky to get a room, for we were only wait-listed. We have come halfway across the world, so we pay the premium for the privilege rather than stay in the village below and trek up again for our second day. It is an ordinary room, but has a shower and toilet. Kit showers and falls asleep the moment his head hits the pillow, but I am to have my own adventure.

First, I find the toilet is not flushing and I take a look. It is a simple ball and hook flush system that has become disconnected. Kit is asleep so I fix it myself. With the water being cloudy it takes me a bit of time. It is a long way to come to do the plumbing, but I certainly would not forget this place!

Li and Kit at Machu Picchu

The advantage of staying at the only hotel at Machu Picchu is to see the ruins at sunrise, at their best, I feel. We would have the place to ourselves, as most tourists do not arrive from the valley on the uncomfortable train until mid-morning.

In the morning we walk part of the Inca trail to the Sun Gate. It is there that the impact of the ruins bursts out at you. Only the very young and fit trekkers hike up the Inca trail and enter the ancient citadel this way, as did the Incas in their glory days. Even the short bit of Inca trail that we walk is not easy, being steep and narrow, with no railings. One slip and it would be goodbye down the mountain side! I am on all fours and Kit has to look after himself. We are lucky and make it back safely. There are Indians with their heavy packs who nimbly go up and down the trail, but we hear that slips and deaths are not uncommon. Often, bodies are not recoverable.

We walk through the ruins again, seeing the bits we missed the day before. We visit the area where the gods were appeased by human sacrifice. Local belief is that evil lurks in such spots, and one should not linger there. In the bright morning light I feel no evil, but after a look at the large flat stones where the victims laid their heads I certainly do not linger! Yet wandering through the ruins with few people around is most appealing; the mountain air, the brightening sky, the songs of birds and scenes of Aztecs warriors in their heyday running through my mind.

Down the mountain and on to the next destination, Yucay, a small Andean village in the Sacred Valley of the Incas. Then it is back to Cusco and the bad news. We learn that the trip to Bolivia has been cancelled as there is political unrest there and strikes at the borders. That means there will be no visit to Lake Titicaca and its floating islands. I had heard the name Titicaca at a geography lesson in Form 1 and said to myself I would like to visit the place one day. Kit knows of my disappointment. He makes inquiries and learns that there is a road to Lake Titicaca. Kit hires a car with a driver. At the hotel we are told that tourists had gone there by car before – an eight hour drive. We smile at each other. Yes, we will take the road trip.

Thus, we travel overnight on the worst road I have ever encountered. It is a cheap four wheel drive for which we paid expensively. We catch the driver falling asleep so Kit offers to drive. Luckily, Kit had some practise with a left-hand drive a few days earlier when our guide fainted. He was taken to hospital and Kit drove the car back to the hotel. So Kit drives while the driver snores away. We follow the road. Some parts of the road are so bad we are travelling over ruts and stones, uphill and downhill, yet the driver sleeps on. He only wakes in the morning as we come to a village, Lake Titicaca in view.

Li and Kit at Lake Titicaca

We are on the water in no time, on a floating island with thatched roof houses. Homes with domestic animals. I think I see a pig. I definitely see chickens running around. Nothing too exciting. Kit is not unhappy, as he can claim to have driven through the night in outback Peru. And I have fulfilled my childhood dream of visiting a faraway place in South America called Lake Titicaca!

Two extremely tired people get back to Sydney, happy to be home, but the trip had burnt a hole in our pockets. A month later we receive a letter sent on behalf of the taxi driver from Peru, who wanted to be further compensated for his hard work driving through the night. His memory is extremely poor. I wish I could have given him a kick!

My most memorable trips I have kept to the end. These were the two trips deeply imprinted into my memory, the first to Cambodia and Vietnam, the other to Turkey. My interest in history has certainly made my travels meaningful, joyful and sorrowful.

Cambodia

The most beautiful sight for me was Angkor Wat at sunset.

As a teenager I came across an article on Angkor Wat and had been intrigued by it since. As a young wife in my twenties I told Kit that it was the one place I wanted to visit. He told me that we did not have the funds, so forget it. What an odd wife he had! All other wives wanted to visit Hong Kong. Cambodia had deteriorated into war by the time we enough money saved. Years of desperate looting and lawlessness in the area followed. Relics from Angkor Wat were looted and many shipped off to the United States.

Almost half a century later I am finally in Angkor Wat. Transfixed, I gaze at the main temple from across a stretch of water. Angkor Wat is a complex of temples, the sacred site of Cambodian Buddhism, more than three times the area of Vatican City. It is sunset, and in the fading light the scene weaves its magic on me. Its beauty leaves me breathless and silent. I am not surprised that others have felt likewise.

126

Angkor Wat

Portuguese friar António da Madalena was an early European visitor in 1586. Awestruck by the extraordinary construction, he later wrote that it was not possible to describe Angkor Wat by pen. Regardless, he went on 'It has towers and decoration and all the refinements which the human genius can conceive of.'

The next morning, back with the small group on this tour, I am equally fascinated. An Englishman and I climb up to the top of a tower. We are able to look into the distance and see how flat the land is. Kit is having problems with his legs. He can manage the flat ground but has difficulty climbing. He also has pains but hides it.

The guide takes us to a part of the complex where the jungle has encroached. The giant roots of trees have wrapped themselves around the sides of the temple. We are taken to where Angelina Jolie was filmed in the movie *Lara Croft: Tomb Raider*. I have got my money's worth and am more than satisfied. We leave Angkor Wat.

Kit and Li with the tour group at Angkor Wat

We have not finished with Cambodia yet. We go on to the capital Phnom Penh and the saddest place of all my tours, the Tuol Sleng Genocide Museum.

I am not quite prepared for what confronts me. I had been told in Machu Picchu that places where people are slaughtered mercilessly retain a certain sense of evil about them. Walking through the rooms at Tuol Sleng, formerly a school, I do not feel a sense of evil. I walk through rows and rows of photographs of prisoners who had been tortured to death. I am shown rooms where the torture had taken place. The beds which still hold the chains, manacles and small instruments used for the purpose of inflicting maximum pain. The guide says that, late at night, people who live in the neighbourhood can hear the anguished cries of pain from those tortured. But it is the sense of emptiness and sorrow that hits me and lingers as I leave the building. Why did Pol Pot and the Khmer Rouge do this to their own people? One answer offered was that their extreme communist ideology made them want to kill.

Vietnam

There is still Vietnam to come. I want to see the country that fought so courageously against foreigners and won.

Firstly, it was for independence from the French. Dien Bien Phu, so much to admire. Local fighters against a heavily fortified force of French soldiers. Military experts of the time considered that the Vietnamese were fighting against the odds. But Ho Chi Minh came through with his men. Men who fought for their country.

I hope that, somehow during our tour, I will get to Dien Bien Phu. It would be such a thrill to see where the fighting took place. But it is not to be. It is too far north and not a tourist spot.

The name of the military strategist had remained with me, Vo Nguyen Giap, a war hero. I chat with the guide while travelling in the coach; he tells me that Giap is still alive but old and poor in health. The government takes care of him and few visitors are allowed. I smile. For me history is never dead or boring. Again, I am proven correct.

Vietnam was to suffer another war, once again against a superior enemy military. The prediction was that they could not prevail against the strongest power in the world. Are the lessons from Dien Bien Phu forgotten?

129

We visit the War Museum in Ho Chi Minh City and there is much to learn about the Vietnam War, or the American War, as they called it in Vietnam. Nearly three million Vietnamese were reported to be killed and four million injured. These are said to be incomplete figures. 58,000 US army men died in the war. I conclude with the words from Robert S McNamara, Secretary of Defence under Presidents Kennedy and Johnson in his memoir *In Retrospect: The Tragedy and Lessons of Vietnam*: 'Yet we were wrong, terribly wrong. We owe it to future generations to explain why.'

I feel that our visit to Vietnam is sad. I leave subdued and morose. But still, one has to rejoice in the resilience of man. Man's triumph in the fight for his beliefs lives through the ages.

Turkey

It is 1997 and I have selected Turkey for our holiday abroad. I tell Kit we should visit somewhere different. I had studied the Roman Empire and Turkey was part of the Eastern Empire. Remember the catchy song *Istanbul (not Constantinople)*? It was a good choice, for it is a lovely country and has special relevance to Australia.

We are taken to Lone Pine and I learn something there.

We walk along the gravestones. There is peace and quiet. One could say that the silence is deafening. It is a beautiful feeling I have never felt before. I am touched by the words inscribed on the Gallipoli Memorial:

'...You, the mothers who send their sons from faraway countries, wipe away your tears; your sons are now lying in our bosom and are in peace, after having lost their lives on this land they have become our sons as well.' Ataturk 1934.

I can relate to Ataturk's words, for although I was born of a different ethnicity and in a different country, Australia is now my home and my country.

The Gallipoli Memorial

Turkey is so beautiful that Kit and I cannot but enjoy ourselves. We visit the Roman ruins – Turkey has a fair share of Roman remnants. We travel on a long stretch of the coast road to Istanbul. The road is smooth and the views great.

We finally arrive in Istanbul. The next morning we visit the famous Blue Mosque, the most beautiful mosque in the world. We go to the Topkapi Palace and museum and are introduced to Muslim art and architecture.

At a night club we see belly dancing by buxom ladies in sequinned costumes. The Sufi (dervish) dancers fascinate me. Their legs move fast as they spin around and their white skirts billow out. Their hands move up and down. While one points upwards to the heavens the other points downwards to earth, the two worlds: the world beyond and the world to which we are chained. The dancers have their eyes closed as they twirl faster and faster, seeking spiritual truth!

Whirling Sufi dancers

I have no problems with the food. We eat eggplant every day, grilled, baked, steamed, fried. No complaints from me. It is my favourite food.

My travels have given me much to be thankful for. The beauty and enchantment of Angkor Wat, the peace of Lone Pine in Gallipoli, the sadness of Tuol Sleng. I feel they have taught me more about life. Too often we want too much and forget what we have already been given.

My days of wine and roses

I was happiest when travelling, visiting countries and learning from them. I felt I received more than other tourists because of my study of history. Knowing something of the background made each country more interesting. Those countries that had to fight for their independence and sacrifice so many lives made them alive for me and not merely statistics. Where there is beauty I am reminded of the genius of man. Where there is inhumanity, atrocity and suffering I am reminded that man's ingenuity could be put to evil use. Too often and too soon the lessons are forgotten as we return to everyday life.

Travel is such a luxury, beyond the reach of so many. But it was never five star travel. I would describe it as three and a half to four stars. Kit and I were too old to backpack and depended on package tours. It did not trouble me that the hotels were simple. They just had to be clean. Sometimes we had to compromise, as we did in India. A colleague of Kit's told us that he had no choice but to go five stars as his wife would not be able to stand the dirt. She also needed her glass of wine. She envied me travelling so often, but I kept mum that our trips cost only half of theirs. Yes, I live simply. I was war baby, growing up during the years when luxuries were few. I do not smoke or drink. I have little jewellery and do not shop much. Kit had been brought up to be thrifty. So I got to travel and looked forward to each trip.

Travelling was not only a feast for my eyes but also for my emotions. I had Kit with me every day for the duration of each trip. I was content that he was near me. I wanted my old age to be spent with him each day and to watch the sunset together. A warm smile from him, as it was when Ah Chieh gave little Li that lovely smile of hers!

Kit did not have many hours at home. He left for work each morning at seven o'clock, as he had far to go, arriving home as it was getting dark each evening. He loved his job. Saturday mornings were spent chasing the little golf ball. Many weekends he was on call. We needed money for the children's private school fees, paying off the home loan, other bills and food to keep us alive. Kit needed funds for his mother to lead a comfortable life. After our first year in Sydney I had to go out to do casual work.. My father's poor health meant he could no longer work. I did not need to send him all my earnings, but my share to help out.

Our trips to Kuala Lumpur were not holidays. As Grace's health deteriorated we went back every year. Each time Kit would kiss and hug Grace, but since Grace and I mutually did not have such feelings we just nodded at each other. Kit often hosted dinners there for Grace and her partner and the relatives. In her heyday, Grace would give long lectures on filial piety and the disrespect of the younger generation for their elders. Of course it was targeted at me. I marvel at how I sat through those sessions. As Kit told his cousin Heng, I was never rude to his mother, I never replied, argued or put on a sour or unpleasant look. Our relationship was always civil. But I am no angel. There were no warm looks, no affection, no play acting. Grace loved flattery and praise. There was none from me. I still hurt intensely from her remarks that I was neither worthy to enter their household nor good enough to be Kit's wife. Because of Grace our relationship was always strained on these visits. I transferred my attention to the local food and the cheap shopping. But I did enjoy seeing my siblings. Anyway, my tastebuds had a great time. Oh, the joys of food!

The 1990s were good years. In 1999 I moved into my dream home. Each morning I woke up happy, each evening I enjoyed the sunset from my bedroom balcony as I gazed at the waters of the Parramatta River flowing past. I expected to spend my old age in this house with Kit and to die here. I loved that house. We owned it outright with no loans, no debts. We were starting to save. We were also helping our children with their home loans.

1999 was my best year. My first grandchild arrived, an absolutely beautiful girl. 2001 was another best year as my second beautiful granddaughter came along. For the next few years there was the sound of little feet and peals of laughter. Yes, those were my years of wine and roses. I learned to enjoy drinking wine and I loved having roses in the house. I had three red rose bushes in the garden.

Red roses were my favourite, although l liked yellow roses too. In our courting days Kit would give me red roses for Valentines Day and my birthday every year without fail. I complained about the cost but did delight in them, trying to keep the blooms alive for as long as I could!

Hard Times: 2010s

Health problems

Kit began to come down with multiple health problems. He had pushed his body to the limit with his golfing, skiing and long hours at work. He called his pains and aches "niggling problems", refusing to accept that they could be more serious. The two pain-killer tablets he swallowed always brought him relief. By 2002 they were becoming less effective, and his shoulders had been troubling him for a while. He presented himself before the shoulder specialist. Could the torn rotator cuffs in both shoulders be repaired? No, he was too old for shoulder surgery. A physiotherapy program was organised instead. This was the beginning; much more was to follow.

Kit coped with a lot of physical pain and was not one to complain. As a result, I did not know the enormity of his problems. Kit was getting increasing pain in his legs and a feeling of weakness. He told me that a spinal operation would "fix" the problem. In 2004 he had his first spinal operation, a major five hour procedure. When he woke on the hospital bed, a pale looking Kit gave me a weak smile and 'See, I told you I will survive.' I was lulled back into the belief that Kit was invincible!

Kit's legs seemed to improve in strength for a while, then the pain and weakness returned. It became worse and Kit insisted on a second spinal operation, another major surgery lasting six hours. Kit woke to smile weakly at a worried-looking wife, again saying 'I told you I will survive!'

Meanwhile, Kit was starting to feel a certain weakness in his hands. His left hand was losing its grip and he could not close his fingers as well as before. He heard that people with bad arthritis had the same problems, so he was consoled and pushed the problem to the back of his mind.

In the years between the spinal surgery Kit developed a swallowing problem. As it worsened, he started choking and coughing at night. The search for a throat specialist started, with the two of us running around the Sydney hospitals, trying to find the reason and a cure. Meanwhile there was a joyful interlude, a very happy occasion for Kit: his surprise 70th birthday party.

The steak dinner party his family said they were taking him to turned out to be a birthday party at the classy golf club where he had enjoyed the game for so many years. I had invited Kit's colleagues, old friends from Malaysia, and golfing mates. My reward for the hard work was to see the happiness on Kit's face. There were friends who Kit had not seen for years. Kit loved company and he loved life, but he had necessarily given up chasing the little white ball and skiing. He now walked more slowly, and his gait was no longer spritely. He still worked, earned a good income and lived a comfortable life.

Unfortunately, among the guests that night were two new acquaintances, known to Kit as "Investment Advisers". Kit liked the younger brother especially. He felt that they meant well and hoped to help earn him a small fortune. It was not that Kit was greedy but took it seriously when told that he was sitting on "equity", as he had a mortgage-free home and savings. His children were struggling with their mortgages, and he wanted to help them. I felt they should not risk their savings but was told that nobody gets rich on a salary and people become affluent through investments. There are also those who lose their savings through bad or ill-advised investments!

The year 2009 was not a good one. Both Grace and Luk May passed away within a fortnight of each other. The new investment was not doing well. The advisers suggested Kit put in more funds by mortgaging the house, which Kit did. He was still working and he and I continued to travel, although we kept a careful watch over our expenses.

Not only had we to pay monthly expenses, but also service the new mortgage. We also started thinking about selling their home, as Kit had thoughts of retirement.

Li and Kit on board for Valentine's Day, 2009

Returning to Sydney Harbour in 2009

And so life continued, not only with Kit's health problems but with financial problems we did not have before.

Kit suggested a big holiday. We wanted a change from the cruising and tours of different countries. Kit's weak legs and constant pain meant a slower lifestyle and fewer outings. We had also been contacting housing agents, but the housing market was down and prices were poor. Kit felt the break was necessary, so I suggested something new: to see wildlife, a safari in South Africa. We were excited as we planned the trip!

On safari

Our African safari in early 2011 was worth doing to see animals in their natural habitat instead of a zoo. During the week in South Africa we saw all the various animals. There were two drives each day, at early sunrise and late in the afternoon. Each outing lasted two and a half hours with a sumptuous tea break. The food was tasty with plenty of meat and home-baked goodies. The fudge was excellent and kept me contented at the back of the special four-wheel drive. It was a great trip.

Kit and Li in Mauritius

Li at the Cape of Good Hope

We packed during the afternoon of our last full day, as we would leave very early the next morning for the drive from Kruger National Park to the airport. But before our departure there was one last drive and a celebration dinner.

We happily climbed into the safari vehicle. We were lucky, for on the way out we saw the "Big Four", on the return stretch spotting the last one, completing the "Big Five" in one afternoon. It was the elephant, lion, rhinoceros, buffalo, and, lastly, the leopard. Even the driver and the guide/tracker were genuinely elated! It was a happy group that returned to the lodge as the sky darkened.

Kit was still exhilarated as he stepped out of the jungle vehicle. Instead of taking the grass path, he walked on the pebble path, slipping on the little stones and falling awkwardly. He jolted his back and bruised his arms and legs. The driver and the tracker helped Kit back to the room and onto the bed. He had no appetite for the special dinner. I was a downcast as I nibbled on the food. Back in our room I found a scented bath with Bougainvillea flowers had been prepared for me by our houseboy. He was a giant young man but most gentle and likeable. The bath was lovely, but we returned to Sydney, Kit limping and I subdued.

Glad to be home, Kit wanted to get into bed, but he had to climb up the stairs to get there. He had only gone about seven steps when one leg collapsed and he fell. His head hit the wall and there he lay, stunned. I got to him and, with much struggle, got him into bed.

The next day Kit rang the departmental head at the hospital to give his resignation.

Kit was a worried man. He had no choice but to resign from a job that he loved, leaving the close-working team that had become almost family and a workplace that was a second home. The body he had pushed beyond its limits could serve him no more. There was too much pain. The house was sold cheaply. There was no choice. We paid off the mortgage and bought an apartment around the corner that was half the price of the house but still had views of the Parramatta River.

My thoughts of spending our last years "on Golden Pond" remained. We still had enough to live a simple life. We could still watch the sunset together. We still had each other. Surely there would be more good times to follow ...

Moving day was a sad one. I remembered the enthusiasm and joy I felt eleven years before when we had moved into my dream home. Giving away possessions to fit into the new, smaller apartment was painful. But there was no time to moan. It was my job to make the place as comfortable and liveable as possible. I had also to learn to make decisions and to say 'No' to an increasingly frail Kit.

Kit had always been the dominant partner and I was happy to sit back and be cared for. Kit was an excellent driver, had attended motor rallies and taken part in cross-country motor runs. But I knew Kit's legs were no longer reliable. Twice of late we had almost gotten into trouble. Both times Kit had veered onto the grass edge and escaped injury, but his leg was too slow at moving to the brake. I was torn. How could I make him give up driving? He had already suffered so much physically and mentally. On retiring he had called himself old and useless, on losing his savings he had blamed himself for being too trusting and careless. Had he checked the particular investment project he would have known it was not viable. His body was in the present state because of his chosen activities. He said he had only himself to blame!

In the apartment Kit continued to fall over, often pulling me down with him. He was a proud man, but he did make one concession: he agreed to use a walking stick. Life moved on. However, we were not pessimistic people. We still kept our sense of humour and looked at the bright side of life. But life had not reached rock bottom.

In early 2015 I started having mild chest pains. Kit made an appointment for me to see the heart specialist, driving me there on the day. I was cleared of any heart problems. It was the stress that was the problem. I expected to go home afterwards, but Kit turned into the shopping centre to buy food, for we needed lunch and fresh meat for dinner.

At the shopping centre Kit found himself a shopping trolley and put his walking stick into it, preferring to push the trolley for some support. And then …

The fall and brain haemorrhage

It all happened so fast. It is around 11:00 am on Tuesday, 13 January 2015. Kit is pushing the shopping trolley with his walking stick in it. I am looking downwards as I walk, but a sudden movement catches my attention. Kit trips as his weak left leg collapses. He falls forwards, his chin hitting the trolley handlebar. He is thrown backwards, his head hitting the concrete floor. He rolls onto his back. His eyes are open, glazed and unmoving. He has lost consciousness and does not respond as I frantically call his name.

141

A female shopper rushes over and turns him onto his side, saying she knows what she is doing. A crowd gathers, and I ask for someone to phone for an ambulance.

After what might have been five minutes Kit's eyes flicker, rest on me and show recognition. Meanwhile security officers from the shopping centre have arrived and set up a screen around us. Kit starts to talk. He knows he had fallen, but not that he had lost consciousness. He says he is alright and asks to go home and be put to bed. He had told me in the past that losing consciousness was a bad sign at any time, so I know he has to go to hospital and be checked out. The ambulance paramedics arrive with a stretcher and I coax Kit onto it. He can see that I will not be persuaded otherwise. I am told that they are headed for Concord Hospital, a familiar place, for I have visited many times when Kit had his swallowing problems. I take the car keys from Kit, retrieve the car from the parking lot and head for the hospital.

Kit arrived at the hospital at 12:20 pm. I find him in the waiting bay. His smile and ability to talk sensibly is reassuring, but I know we could be in trouble. We are both calm. Years with Kit have taught me to be calm and rational, not the emotional mess I had been when we first met.

An hour later he is given a bed in the observation ward. He has been able to contact our daughter and youngest son to tell them what has happened. I sit next to his bed and conduct my own observations. Kit tries to reassure me that all is well. He reminds me that he is a survivor.

At 2:45 pm Kit's speech starts to slur. At 3:00 pm he starts to vomit. I run to the doctors to tell them. At 3:20 pm Kit is wheeled into X-Ray for a brain scan. The scan shows massive bleeding in the brain. At 3:45 pm he is rushed into the operation theatre for an emergency brain operation. At 4:00 pm Kit is operated on.

I am told that the operation will take some three and a half to four hours. The medical registrar is most kind. They have

142

learnt that Kit was one of them. In fact, the young anaesthetist has recognised Kit as having helped train him. I learn later that he had told this to the surgeon. They were worried that he might be a casualty on the operating table but would do their best. I go home, less than 15 minutes away, and jot down everything that has happened that morning, as I do on the following days.

I return at 8:00 pm that evening with my youngest son. At 9:30 pm we are allowed to have a quick look at him. He is wired up to a whole lot of machines and in an induced coma.

Next morning at the hospital I am directed to the Intensive Care Unit. It is the same scene as the night before. I am advised not to return that day as he will still be in an induced coma. So Wednesday passes.

On Thursday I am allowed to sit next to his bed. Morning passes. Evening comes. There is a flickering of the eyelids, but they do not open. Another day passes.

On Friday there is more flickering of the eyelids. I talk to Kit, telling him I am his wife and that he has had a bad fall. Softly, I say that I am waiting for him to say hello to me. The afternoon passes and it starts to get dark.

Kit turns to me, still sitting next to his bed. He says hello, the first words since his operation. I am elated that he seemed to recognise me, as I have been told the brain damage can include up to 50% loss of memory.

Over the days the registrar there, Dr Choong, has spoken to me twice, each time about the dire consequences of the damage to Kit's brain. He tells me that the doctors had not expected Kit to survive the operation as the bleeding had been massive. Had they operated ten minutes later it would have been too late – Kit had been centimetres away from death. His survival did not mean all was well. Memory loss was nothing compared to other problems, loss of speech, physical movement and worst still, he could be a "vegetable". At that stage I am not prepared to let Kit go. Whatever state he is in I want him next to me and to be able to just touch him.

On Sunday, my nephew – Yeh's son – and his wife fly in from Melbourne. They remembered that Kit and I had flown to see Yeh when he suffered a major stroke some years ago. Yeh was still fragile in health and could not make the trip to Sydney.

I am sitting next to Kit when they come walking towards us. Kit recognises them and there is much joy in the reunion. Kit is still wired to a machine and wears a mask. While they talk to Kit, Yeh's wife notices that Kit has raised his right hand, the first movement from his right side, which had been paralysed after the fall. Another improvement, another step forwards. I take the visitors out to a good Chinese lunch, returning afterwards to the hospital. Then it is time for them to drive to the airport and fly back to Melbourne. Their visit is soothing for me. It has been a good day.

As the days pass Kit becomes more responsive and seems to remember more. Kit is even able to comfort me, telling me not to be sad. That he is improving and he is well! On Tuesday, exactly a week after entering hospital, he is transferred from Intensive Care to the Neurological ward.

A second week drags past in the new ward. Kit is not as closely watched. I have to run to the nurses' desk when whenever he needs to move his bowels, as he needs to be lifted by the big machines. I cannot help but laugh when the doctor asks why he is having tummy upsets. Does he not realise that Kit is not allowed outside food, that everything comes from the hospital kitchen?

A third week passes. Kit is still very weak but there has been improvement. The registrar tells me that Kit's recovery has been remarkable. Kit complains about headaches but still we are able to watch TV together. We see an exciting match

144

between Kyrgios and Murray, as the Australian Tennis Open is on. Kit is starting to smile as friends turn up to visit.

Kit is transferred from the Concord Hospital to the Metropolitan Rehabilitation Hospital at Petersham for six weeks rehabilitation.

I commute to the rehabilitation centre every day, arriving at 10:00 am and leaving before it gets dark. Kit has lost 10 kilos, down to 60 kilos. One day in the lift, travelling to the gym, his short pants slip down. It is okay as he wears diapers.

Kit is still frail and weak, but his days are cheered by his many visitors. Kit is a people-lover and is popular. I cannot be bothered to make lunch and snack on the goodies the visitors bring. I am most annoyed when I am late one morning and a visitor from Kit's workplace has eaten up half the treats there. However, I get to share Kit's lunch, as his appetite is still poor.

At the rehabilitation centre there are jobs that the patient's family members are expected to do. For Kit, this includes taking him to another hospital for a nerve conduction test.

I think Kit benefits most from the daily physiotherapy sessions. They help to strengthen his limbs and the physiotherapist trains him to use the walker, good for his mobility.

However, while the care is good, accidents still happen. Early one morning I get a call. Kit has been found on the floor of his room. He had tried to use the walker to get to the toilet but slipped and fell. Luckily, his face had fallen onto a book, The V.I. Anthology by CM Chung, which had cushioned the fall and he was found soon after it happened. He suffered no ill effects, unlike the unlucky incident of neglect in 2020 at an aged care home that led to a collapsed lung and Kit's subsequent death!

Kit has been in the rehabilitation centre for a month when we find the local politics affecting us. The Centre wants Kit out as soon as possible, as they need to show results to the government, including rapid recovery and turnover of patients. They assure me that there are aged care centres that can continue their good work.

Kit is not fit enough to move out. It is my honest opinion. I beg them to keep him a while longer, but my pleas fall on deaf ears.

☯

In early March the decision-makers recommend a 10 week package for home care. The home package turns out to be full of holes!

The charade starts with profuse congratulations to Kit for his fantastic recovery. The Centre washes its hands of him. On 18 March Kit is given his discharge papers, five days earlier than originally planned. Kit is unhappy that he has not been given time to say goodbye and thank the workers who have been so kind and helpful to him. Kit and I have to leave our presents behind, since we cannot personally hand them over. I am unhappy because I am convinced that Kit would benefit from another fortnight there. But who am I? Who is Kit?

Meanwhile, on the home front, renovations have been taking place. The step in the bathroom has been removed, creating a flat space and a new shower area, and handrails have been installed.

The kitchen, which had been badly neglected by the previous owner, is renovated to a cheerful, bright and attractive place, although still small. As usual costs turn out far more than the estimates.

The home package workers are often late or don't show up. I take over the showering, as the last worker was massively overweight and could not bend over. The exercise person was a health worker, not a physiotherapist. She was most pleasant but inexperienced, and overestimated Kit's abilities, leading to two falls, which, although not serious, were painful for Kit.

I retain the cleaning services and social support. The woman sent to provide social support was with Kit for four years.

I take Kit back to see his neurological surgeon for his post-operative consultation. This surgeon is a very kind person. He tells me that when he was drawing blood from Kit's brain he had expected the worst. Kit's recovery was the most satisfying case in his whole career and had made him feel that he had chosen the right profession. He tells Kit that he is looking at a miracle and to spend his time wisely, as it is borrowed time!

2015: I am in trouble – an email brings bad tidings

'Li has a dark past, an almost evil nature ... she must be punished', says cousin Heng from Kuala Lumpur.

I had emailed Kit's cousin Heng to inform him that Kit has had a bad accident, that Kit suffered a cerebral haemorrhage. I cannot believe what I read in the return email. It is a letter circulated to Kit's friends and relatives, an attack on my character. 'Li has a dark past, an almost evil nature ... she needs to be punished.' A list of my "crimes": bad mouthing her mother-in-law for 52 years, refusal to obey mother-in-law since marriage, in recent months bad mouthing sister-in-law, in refusing to forgive mother-in-law after her death in 2009, she has hurt and harmed Kit. Besides, in earlier years she has forced her husband to obey her and go against his mother.

It is May 2015. Kit is back from the rehabilitation hospital, but still recovering from his injuries. He wakes in the late morning and finds me crying. I have just read the email from Heng and am troubled. Heng has appealed to Kit to take his side against me. Will Kit take his cousin's side? Heng expects it because he is a blood relative. Their fathers were brothers, in fact Heng's father was the eldest brother, so he is almost an elder brother himself!

Cousin Heng feels his importance. He attended Kit and my engagement dinner and wedding luncheon. He is a doctor and well respected in Kit's extended family. At 80 years of age he is the most important and senior member of that family. I had not taken well to him when we first met. He had small eyes and a hard look. But I told herself I should not judge others by their looks. It was unfair and we do not have a choice, as we are born with what we have. Still, he would make a first class villain! He had wormed himself into my good books one evening at an informal extended family pot luck dinner. He called me aside and said he was aware that I was having a hard time with Grace. I could hardly believe my ears. I thought I had found a friend for life!

Meanwhile Kit found he and Heng had something in common. Heng had a beautiful golf swing, hitting unbelievable distances. So Heng came to visit in Sydney and play golf.

Heng was from a conservative Buddhist family and very traditionally Chinese. He made few concessions in life, but that was his own business and nothing to do with me. Both Kit and I noticed that he had unhealthy habits. I placed extra spoons on all the dishes for lunch or dinner. Heng ignored them and continued to plunge his chopsticks right into the middle of the dish. If I told him not to do that he would 'lose face.' He was his own person, for he had dared tell me that Grace was a pompous and difficult person. 'Pompous Bella Donna' was my nickname for Grace, although I did not mention it to anyone.

Heng came to Sydney for a second golf visit. His habits would never change. I continued to play the gracious hostess. Meanwhile I learnt that Heng had a partner. With his plain looks and lack of charm, he had not been successful in his pursuit of girls when young. He was only interested in attractive and well-educated ones. However, in his late forties he showed a change in taste, and his partner was half his age. I kept his secret. I felt that we all have a right to our choices. On his third visit he brought his partner, who was indeed a very pleasant fellow. Again I tried my best to give them a good time.

Back to May 2015. I found the vicious attack hard to understand. Perhaps it was his new religious zeal that motivated him to act the way he did – he was newly converted from Buddhism to Catholicism. But then again, the Christian religion warns against judging and punishing others, even wrongdoers; to leave it to God.

Heng's plan was to circulate the email to close friends living in Sydney to let them know that I am evil and cannot be allowed to look after Kit. He believed a group could be formed. They could then wrest hold of Kit and Kit's finances and kick me out. This was the due punishment for me. Heng was neither practical nor successful with his plans, for who would spend time fighting for a sick and crippled man unless there was love?

I am touched by Kit's defence. He accuses Heng of a vicious attack on his 75 year old wife and attempt to break up a 55 year marriage. Kit tells Heng that he has little understanding of family life. That although I did not get along with Grace, I had always been respectful. There had been no emotional confrontations, accusations, or the use of strong language between the women. It was wrong to say I was guilty of bad-mouthing.

I had never complained to relatives or family friends about Grace. As for Chun, I got along with her, often staying with her for short holidays in Singapore. Heng refuses to stop attacking me. Heng insults Kit, insisting I am different to what he believes me to be, that he has been bullied and subdued. Wow, I deserve an Oscar for 55 years of outstanding acting! Kit fires back again that Heng has little idea or knowledge of married life.

That ended their correspondence and we never saw Heng again.

I felt sad when I thought of Heng or reflected on this incident. He had stayed with us and seen that we were a happy couple. Why did he hate me? I had always treated him well, yet Heng had tried to reach across the ocean from Malaysia to Australia to punish me. However, I had been an Australian citizen for 35 years, subject to Australian laws, not outdated Chinese traditions.

To Heng, I was not of Kit's family. I was a Zhang, an outsider and a female, unimportant, only a person to be punished. I was expected to be submissive and to accept my punishment. But Heng did not know me. I have never been the submissive traditional Chinese woman of the last century. I am a fighter. Even if he had been swayed by Heng, I was never going to give up caring for Kit. Heng did not understand love. I will always fight for whom and what I believe in.

The Mother: Self-reflection

I love my children, although I now realise I had been negligent.

Life in Australia was physically taxing for me. I had not had to cook or keep house in Malaysia and was conscious that I am not strongly built. There were times when I was just exhausted from my home duties. From the beginning, Kit had wanted me to be responsible for running the household and disciplining the children. He worked long hours to pay the children's private school fees and the mortgage. He was also a very sociable person, surrounded by friends and enjoying their company when he was not at the hospital.

I, too, did paid work, sometimes five days a week, as I felt an obligation to help my parents financially. They were my responsibility, not Kit's. Besides, I didn't want to give Grace the opportunity to boast that Kit was helping to support his in-laws, another potential matter to hold against me. I feared too much. Yet Luk May, my mother, at one of the gatherings of our returned visits to Malaysia, had thanked Grace for Kit's generosity in helping them. The funds had come from my earnings and not from Kit! Luk May was so silly and humble. Again, I learnt that you can control yourself but not what others say or do.

I must admit that I did not know how to openly give love, self-assurance and encouragement to my children. My own parents never gave of themselves and the adult who did give me love, Ah Chieh, left me at eleven years of age. I had no role model when dealing with children and had little confidence. I had grown up thinking of myself as being of little worth, and could not be both a dedicated wife and mother. So I did not make myself readily available to my daughter and sons. I was not the easy-going, smiling and patient mother, full of smiles and hugs. Kit was my priority and had first call on my time. Only with Kit was I ready to laugh and give of myself.

151

There was plenty of love within me but I did not have the maturity to understand and balance my obligations.

To make matters worse, I had allowed myself to be governed by fear, not wanting to be like Grace and dominate or hurt my children or, later, their spouses. I felt I could end up making such demands on them, so I erected a barrier to protect them and myself!

Further, I wanted my children to learn mental and emotional strength so they could fend for themselves. They had more of these qualities than I had as a child, so they should be able to cope, I thought. By the time I was eighteen I was over-sensitive, my mind fragile and brittle. I had learnt bitterness. Not my children, or so I thought.

All of our children had suffered abuse and racism at school in Australia, although they had not complained of it to me or Kit at the time. My eldest son and daughter were quiet and serious. My youngest son also. I had ill-prepared them for life, just as I had not been prepared.

Our second son stole hearts with his huge eyes and appealing smile. He was the child who did not hesitate to approach me, while his siblings were serious and shy. He had the Zhang family eyes and his father's face. As a child of eight he had spoken up for me one day when I was dispirited. He told Kit that his grandmother did not like me, while she liked him and his siblings because they were her grandchildren. Kit took it as a sign of disrespect for his mother and lashed out at him. With tears in his eyes our son had looked to me for support. I was too cowardly and failed him as well. To jump to his support would have ended in a quarrel between Kit and me.

Victoria Institution Global Reunion October 2015

I still have much to do. I help Kit recover as best he can. We still have friends around us. There are outings for an occasional lunch or dinner or a visit to the casino. Then I receive news of the school reunion in Singapore for alumni of the Victoria Institute, taking place in October 2105. This event is already described in *The Reluctant Migrant's Daughter*. This, I think, is the ideal trip, for the many younger schoolmates can surely help Kit to move around.

The VI had become a shadow of what it had been, but the students of old never forgot the school that they loved.

This reunion of the VI alumni is the most successful ever organised. It is well-planned and executed. Many of the attendees are in their fifties and sixties, some in their seventies like me at 75 and Kit at 78. A few even older. Kit is the first to attend in a wheelchair.

With much effort Kit can stand and take a few steps. He is frail but when he flashes his smile the boyishness and mischievous look return to his face. I feel I am healthy and fit and am determined to ensure that life is still worth living for Kit.

The reunion is a happy time for both Kit and me. I am overjoyed to see a few familiar faces, especially old schoolmate CM Chung, the school historian. We were year mates and the same age. I had been only in the school for my two final years, while the male students were there for up to seven years. As expected, the schoolmates rally to help Kit. They piggyback him into and out of the bus, seat him on his wheelchair and help push him around. Because of their help, Kit is able to enjoy the tours of Singapore. We visit all the planned highlights, the Gardens by the Bay, the Maritime Xperiential Museum (which focused on Zheng He, a favourite historical figure of mine), Chinatown and Little India.

The organisers have not forgotten the food either. We visit the ever-popular Hawkers Food Stalls on the first night. On another evening we dine on seafood at a venue on the shoreline.

The grand finale is the Gala Dinner Night. The school captains of old are called to the stage and honoured. Kit is wheeled there and carried on to the stage to sit with the others.

The saddest and sweetest moments come with the singing of the songs. The school song is sung earlier in the evening, before dinner and the speeches. It is sung with gusto, but behind the loud voices is a sadness and an aching memory of a beautiful past. A question lingers … will there be another reunion, will we meet again? Then the program for the evening begins. There is the entertainment followed by speeches, reminiscences by the speakers, songs by the members and finally a magic show.

At midnight there is a final farewell to the strains of Auld Lang Syne. It is such a sad tune that many of the ladies are in tears, as in my case. It is another gathering for the reluctant migrants who left Malaysia so many years ago.

Life Goes On: 2016 - 2017

The reunion of Victoria Institute alumni in Singapore leaves us happy. We carry on with life in Sydney, although physically it is a struggle. Kit does not complain and lives with his pains. I aim to give Kit a good life, and since he has always been active I plan a trip to the USA.

Cruising there and back would be the solution. I am more experienced in looking after Kit now and will be able to manage him. Also, I have developed stronger arms and am no longer shy to ask for help when I see strong-looking males! Kit is always cooperative and makes every effort physically. The journey to the USA is pleasant, and we enjoy the food and shows on the ship.

A different ship is to return us to Sydney, so we take a taxi to the port just over the border in Canada.

At the wharf we are greeted by a representative from the ship. The ship is docked just metres away. I ask him to look after Kit, who is standing, while I help the taxi driver to unload the luggage. For some reason best known to this person, he fails to hold Kit, who falls forward. The man makes no attempt to stop the fall, but the driver sees Kit falling, dashes forward and catches him. I have met another Good Samaritan and cannot thank him enough!

Back in Sydney, Kit's close group of ex-colleagues visit, and they are back to their lunch outings. Come 31 December, Kit and I are at the home of good friends, Percy and Cherry, to watch the New Year's Eve fireworks and welcome in 2017. They were fellow travellers and golfers, who we are most fortunate to have as friends.

2017 is a good year. The highlight is Kit's 80th birthday. The celebration is at Kit's old golf club again, but small compared to his 70th ten years before. It is a happy evening for Kit. He has two sons with him, his daughter and three grandchildren, plus some 35 guests. Kit feels blessed and is thankful.

There is yet another treat waiting. At the end of the year our second son joins us on a cruise to New Zealand. His wife has taken a trip back to South America. Second son is a sportsman, strong and active. He helps me to shower and dress his father each morning. Consequently, I am less tired and more relaxed. I could not ask for a better holiday. We wine and dine well and there is much laughter.

In the meantime I discover respite care. I find I can have a short visit back to Kuala Lumpur, leaving Kit in an aged care home. I can recharge my batteries and rest the bad back and aching shoulders I have developed. I can also take four days off just to have a break and visit Kit once a day. Most of all, I enjoy the sense of freedom.

Old Age and Love

The old lady sees not

The frail crippled old man,

Half-bald but still left with wispy white hair.

Age has lined his face,

Yet as he smiles, the years fade away.

The smile is the same of olde,

She sees the young man, vital and strong,

With thick black hair and glowing skin ...

She lifts her face and with misty eyes she returns to
the present.

The wispy white hair is soft, especially near the ears.

The old lady loves to touch it.

No one can withstand the ravages of time

But where there is love there is a difference.

Love has no limits.

It lives and grows.

It colours what we see.

It gives beauty and peace to

Those who want it and have it ...

2018: A Sad Year

Tears

Weep, weep for all you want

Tears bring relief to the human soul.

Tears help you to carry on with life

To go forwards with what you believe in.

Pity those who cannot weep

Who have no time for tears

Who life has traumatised so deeply

That tears do not flow anymore.

For tears are like the rain

The sudden deluge, the tropical storm

Or just the normal rain.

The rain lifts the suffocating heat

And replaces it with the gentle breeze and cool air,

It brings a sense of renewal,

It cleanses and washes away the dirt,

The plants receive the life sustaining water.

Like the rain, tears allow the person to face life anew.

My last argument with Kit

My last argument with Kit was in 2018, an event I did not understand until after his death. It was also the last time I visited "dark places". We did not quarrel often and I would be very upset each time. Once Kit tried to console me. He told me that quarrels are part of married life and I should not be so sensitive.

Again, it was over Grace, although she had gone many years ago. My usual silly self, I never seemed to learn. I had stupidly stated that Grace was not always honest in relation to past incidents. It caught Kit at a bad time. He was furious and truly gave it to me.

He told me that I fabricated things about his mother. That they were untruths. He claimed that she never did or said the things I had accused her of. Stupid Li had always been blunt and honest while Grace had always prefaced her criticisms as gentle advice to help Li.

I could not believe my ears. Is that what he thinks of me after fifty-six years of marriage and some sixty years of being together? So I am a liar? I was absolutely devastated. I moved around in a daze for the next two days, saying little.

I had been dealt a heavy blow. I have my principles. Love never dies ... but something in me snapped. I finally accepted that his mother came first. I never brought up her name again.

I felt a certain detachment. I no longer worshiped Kit as I used to, finally accepting that he was human and had his faults and weaknesses. Although to me he was still an outstanding person and a very loveable person at that.

No, I would never stop caring for him. To put him in a nursing home and cut myself free never entered my thoughts. To do so I would lose my self-respect, my values and my beliefs. Perhaps the detachment was necessary so I could continue to look after him, with some cleaning help from the aged care people. It made me more practical and accepting that life could be harsh.

In 2023 I realised something I had forgotten in 2018. I was still the romantic person, while Kit had lost almost half his memory and part of his ability to reason. Our earliest memories are our strongest, and these would be of his mother. Mine are of Ah Chieh, who had shown me love. Much of the memory Kit lost would probably be those of his happy days with me! He was no longer a fully functional, rational person. He would not have wanted to hurt me.

So I go through 2018 a more practical and tougher person. I stop feeling guilty for going away and leaving Kit in respite care. I now feel that I owe it to myself. Yet I do still care.

Kit is weakening further and he is not as chatty as before. The doctors did warn me that he will deteriorate further, physically and mentally, not just due to ageing, but to the damage he suffered from his fall.

On Thursdays throughout 2018, Stella from the aged care service comes over and we all go out for lunch. We are starting to struggle to transfer Kit into and out of the car. I suspect it is me who is weakening, with my bad back and shoulders. Kit never complains, even when we drop him once. His gentle smile is always there.

I also learn something from the staff at the respite centre: Kit counts the days until I return to take him home. His joy grows as the day nears! He has always been a lovable person.

The disaster cruise: 2018

Memories of last year's cruise lingers in my mind. Kit, our second son and I had such an enjoyable time! I am greedy for a repeat and second son also wants to do it again. But life is not generous.

160

I book the same cruise to New Zealand for the three of us in a single suite. It is a quiet holiday for a sick man, his elderly wife and a caring son. It is not meant to be a merrymaking, boisterous holiday of fun and noise. Second son's wife and their child also book a cabin on the cruise.

The first evening passes peacefully. Tired from the flight to Auckland, we all sleep well. Our son helps me shower Kit the next morning but rushes off, leaving me to dress him. He is worried about his wife and child and has gone to check on them.

I know that our son would prefer to be with his wife and child. Since they were on the ship, I feel I should give them as much time together to enjoy the cruise and I will look after Kit as much as I can. If a mother loves her son she must be willing to make sacrifices.

As the first evening goes well, I am lulled into complacency, dropping my guard in looking after Kit. On the second evening disaster strikes!

Being in a suite, we have access to a smaller, more exclusive dining room with its own menu and wines. Kit has been longing for a steak and orders one, but first we enjoy our pre-dinner drinks at the bar. Kit's steak arrives and he goes to the table, where the waiter slices it up for him. I finish my drink and move to the table. The pieces of steak are far too large; I normally cut Kit's meat into small pieces. Too late, Kit has popped a large piece into his mouth and, with inadequate chewing, swallows it. He starts choking and gasping for air!

I witness one of the most horrifying scenes in my life. Right before my eyes Kit's lips start to turn blue. A diner at the next table witnesses what is happening. He dashes over, applies the Heimlich procedure, pinning Kit's arms backwards and thumping his back to dislodge the meat. The piece of meat goes down and colour returns to Kit's face. His lips turn pink once more. Son and I call out to him. He smiles at us, reassuring us he is alright. Another Good Samaritan has helped us.

Son and I take him back to the suite and put him to bed. He sleeps well, but I do not, watching him for the greater part of the night. The next day is quiet and Kit is made to rest.

He seems back to normal.

On the fourth morning we reach Wellington. There are buses waiting to take passengers to town. I feel that I need to be by myself for a while. A bus ride will be good for me. My son and family decide to stay onboard, so I ask them to look after Kit for a couple of hours. I will meet them for early buffet lunch.

They are indeed early for lunch and have plates of food when I find them. I look at Kit's plate. He has selected two pieces of sweet corn and Indian food, as well as some salad. I have yet to get my food, but am happy to watch him eat, telling him to go slow. He takes a small spoonful of curry and starts coughing. The spices irritate his throat. Kit does cough, more often at night, something our son does not know. He has not forgotten the choking incident and pesters me to allow him to take Kit to see the ship's doctor. Another mistake! He does not know that the consultation fees are exorbitant and there is little they can do: band-aid solutions, perhaps cough mixtures and antibiotics for the standard patients.

He also does not know that we have made expensive visits to the ship's doctor on previous cruises. Two years earlier Kit fell, as his wheelchair struck a small lump of wires under the carpet. I could have gone to see the captain over the issue but had not wanted to be a source of trouble. Kit's fall was not serious but I had to pay expensively for the 45 minutes he was kept under observation in the medical clinic. Likewise, I had to pay for the gastroenteritis I got from eating the buffet salad! But I do not want to appear miserly and am too tired to argue. He goes ahead while I help myself to a small plate of food and some fruits for my lunch.

The ship's doctor is a lady in her early thirties. She has such a pleasant and sweet face that I trust her and want to believe that she will help a fellow doctor. Afterwards, it dawned on me that her loyalties were with those who buttered her bread. Kit was a possible source of trouble. His medical problems were beyond her should they flare up. We had docked at Wellington and the city presented her with the ideal opportunity to get rid of him!

I think the doctor lied to our son. She told him that Kit had aspiration pneumonia, and Kit should go to Wellington Hospital for checking, but WOULD BE ALLOWED TO RETURN TO THE SHIP if he was cleared. She would arrange for the ambulance.

I refuse our son's offer to accompany us. I tell him to stay onboard and I will keep in touch. It is suggested that I pack a little bag.

At the hospital we are met by the ship's agent. She is most helpful. At the hospital they are helpful too. On learning that Kit was a doctor they attend to him immediately. He is put through various tests. At 6:00 pm Kit is medically cleared and ready to be discharged. The agent is still with me. I request that she contact the ship to let them know we are ready to continue the cruise and ask her to help arrange for us to be picked up at the next port of call. It was then that she tells me, out of pity, that the ship is never going to take us back. She makes the appeal but knows that the answer will be in the negative.

Yes, cruises have a dark side that passengers do not always know!

But our ordeal has not ended. The agent tells me I have no choice. I beg the hospital to keep Kit for the night. The agent books me into a hotel across the road and offers to take me to the airline office to book tickets for a flight back to Sydney. I return to the hospital to tell Kit of the developments and, as usual, he accepts what I say with a smile.

The only flight with two seats left is not until 4:00 pm. We take a taxi to the airport and I say goodbye to Wellington and our misadventures in New Zealand. Yet there is one more surprise. We get Kit onto the plane but find no male steward to transfer him from the wheelchair to his seat. The attractive, smiling female stewards tell me that it is my problem, not theirs. Then another steward steps forward to help. She lifts Kit by the shoulders while I lift his lower body. I close my eyes, say a prayer, and, with every ounce of my strength, lift Kit onto the plane seat. Amazed at myself, but exhausted, we sit through the flight back to Sydney.

Back home, Kit asks me where his white pants are. I told him they were soiled and dirty and I had left them in the bin in the hotel. 'Oh no, I had $160 Australian dollars in the pocket. Did you not check?'

Return to Malaysia

The Disaster Cruise had not only cost us financially. Now my back gives me pain and so does my right shoulder. I explain to Kit that I need rest and he nods vigorously in agreement. Even with the brain damage he can understand, and he is willing to go into respite care for a week, although he would have preferred to stay at home.

Once I have recovered, my mind goes into overdrive again. Second son has read some articles praising the virtues of Penang Island, off the northwest coast of Malaysia. It is described as an ideal place, both beautiful and peaceful. I had made two short visits to the state of Penang but do not know it well. Our son thinks maybe that is the place to which we should retire. We can rent a house and employ a housekeeper cum cook and a local nurse to help Kit. Labour is much cheaper there. Kit and I can live out our days there and not be separated. Our savings will probably be enough, say, for another seven years. The only problem is medical care, but it is worth a try, at least for a few months before we decide: we can always come home to Australia.

I am realistic enough to know that we cannot continue to live in our apartment together without help. I am in my late seventies, too weak to look after Kit. We do not have the funds for private nursing care in Australia. Kit does not want to go into aged care and I cannot bear to see an unhappy Kit. My duty and love are for him.

Second son feels strongly that Malaysia may be the solution. We can come back to visit Sydney. He offers to take a week off to help us settle in. He finds us a large apartment and a carer with some medical experience to look after Kit. He will return after three months to check on us. If we are unhappy we will return to Sydney.

In March 2019 we fly out of Sydney, setting foot on Malaysian soil again after 42 years.

What one plans and visualises often turns out to be different from reality. The beautiful island of Penang turns out to be a sleepy hollow with few interesting places. The strong Australian dollar is disappointing, as the cost of living in Malaysia has gone up and labour is no longer cheap. It is not the promised paradise!

It has been a tiring trip, with a long wait in transit for the connecting flight to Penang. However, it is a beautiful sunny morning that greets our arrival. The carer for Kit, Cora, in her thirties and with her generous smile, is already waiting for us at the apartment building's lounge downstairs. She is strongly built, healthy-looking and speaks English. She is a Filipina.

We are taken up to our apartment by the housing agent. It is airy and attractive, with a huge sitting room. From the large balcony we can see the sea in the distance. We had been told that we were by the sea. Apparently that was ten years ago, before the land reclamation projects. There go our walks next to the water!

We feed Kit and put him to bed. There is much to do to settle in. The place is extremely dusty and we are lucky to find a cleaner that day and get her to clean the place. Second son is with us for the week and he goes to work immediately. Firstly, we sort out the food problem. There are many caterers around. Prices are reasonable and the food is tasty. We have dinner catered, while lunch is to be selected from the food courts around us. On the fifth floor of our multi-storied apartment is a food court. With four lifts to service the building it takes me around five minutes to get there. The complex just next door has no apartments but a dozen food outlets, some ten restaurants and numerous other shops. We certainly would not starve!

Our son helps us shop for household items, including a good armchair in which Kit can watch TV comfortably. It is a busy but happy week. Soon our son has gone, back to work and his family in Sydney.

Life has changed in Malaysia. Domestic work is unpopular. The younger women prefer factory jobs. Pay rates have also gone up steeply. Live-in help is hard to find, even day help is no longer nine to five but paid by the hour, with a maximum of 6 hours. The room at the back of the apartment is shabby, only good enough to use as a storage room. The apartment has two other bedrooms besides the large master bedroom. I need to have a good, comfortable room for Cora, as I want her to be healthy and well to look after Kit. I also need a good guest room for family and friends to use when they visit. I give up looking for a live-in housekeeper.

We enter our second week in Penang. Cora turns out to be a good worker. She is able to get Kit to do his morning exercises. Kit is able to push his walker from the bedroom to the dining room. Cora hates cooking, and hard-boiled eggs is all she will do. Our breakfast is simple, bread and jam, but also tasty local cakes. I either buy lunch and bring it home or Cora pushes Kit in his wheelchair to the food outlets in the next building.

However, Cora has an accident while manoeuvring Kit out from the bathroom after his morning shower.

I am in the sitting room when I hear a loud bang and rush into the master bedroom. Kit is in his overturned wheelchair just outside the bathroom. Cora had slipped, grabbed Kit's wheelchair and he was thrown backwards, with the back of his head hitting the floor. Cora and I set the wheelchair upright. I look at Kit's head. A huge lump has come up. He looks stunned, but recovers quickly and assures us he is alright. His first words are 'I am alright, it is an accident.' Cora is in tears and apologises profusely. I tell Cora to phone for a taxi. We are going to the private hospital not far from the apartment. I have to make sure that Kit is not injured.

The wait for the neurologist is under an hour, then Kit is put through some tests. The neurologist is of the opinion that Kit is alright, but since there is a head knock it is best to keep

167

him in hospital overnight for observation. He assures me that Kit is not in trouble. Cora offers to stay the night with him. That morning our first visitors from Singapore had arrived: my best friend and her sister-in-law had come for a two-day visit. I manage to see them for diner that evening.

Early the next morning my visitors go sightseeing and I go to the hospital to see Kit. He is considered fit and is discharged. Kit is happy to meet up with my visitors and we have the evening meal together. Then it is goodbye to the visitors the next day. I enjoyed their short stay – they were such a comfort to have around, especially after Kit's accident.

More visitors. I have invited the next couple because I feel sorry for the wife. She was Kit's secretary during the years he worked in Ipoh. Timid, shy and introspective, but absolutely loyal. Each time we visited Malaysia she would attempt to see Kit. She and her husband come for a weekend. I try to give her a good time but it is not easy. At dinner it is difficult selecting dishes, as she has a lot of food taboos. Sometimes it happens with elderly Buddhists. They abstain from certain meats, such as beef and lamb, and certain vegetables too.

On the second afternoon I come out from my room to find our guests taking photos of the family photos displayed in the sitting room. She wants to put them on Facebook. I have to inform her we want no publicity and do not want our privacy invaded. She is hurt and I feel guilty. That is the last time we see her. Sometimes it is hard to please everybody.

Our next visitors are family and we have a lovely time. It is my sweet younger granddaughter and her delightful boyfriend, Owen. We take them to see the sights and enjoy the special cuisine, the spicy Peranakan food. Meanwhile, I had discovered a nearby market where I found delicious local fruits, including jackfruit and durian. Kit and I have been enjoying the durian. Owen takes to it as well. The smell of the fruit does not put him off and he agrees that it melts in your mouth. We appreciate the fruity red wine Owen brought. We enjoy the stories he tells us about growing up in Saudi Arabia. All too soon they are gone.

A month later our daughter turns up for a five day stay. It is also a joyful time for us. She sees her father to bed and when he wakes in the morning. It is precious quality time that can be devoted to her father without the distractions of work and children. Under the same roof, it is like old times. It was the same when our second son was with us. Our youngest is to visit soon. It is happy days again! There is a good gym and swimming pool at the apartment and our daughter is delighted with the facilities.

Our final visitor is Boon, a fellow teacher of mine and an occasional fellow golfer of Kit's. His son drove him and wife from Ipoh. Boon's vision has deteriorated but his wife is even less fortunate. She has early dementia but can respond to him, and he looks after her. The couple stay with us while their son stays with friends . He comes each day to take us out. We get to see the surrounding areas of Penang, which they know better than Kit and me. We are taken to the huge Buddhist temple, which is quite a distance from our place.

We eat at a seafood restaurant next to the shore and see the harbour lights. The most humorous incident of their visit is yet to take place!

On the last afternoon, an hour after lunch, Boon is dashing around looking for his wife. I am in the sitting room, while Kit is in bed for his afternoon nap. Cora is in her room.

No, I have not seen Boon's wife. She is not in the guest room or in the sitting room, not in the kitchen or the back of the apartment. Boon does not think she could have darted out of the apartment. We ask Cora to help us search for her. A few minutes later Cora calls out from the master bedroom. There, lying next to a soundly sleeping Kit, is Boon's wife. She is curled up on my side of the bed, with my blanket covering her and tightly hugging my second pillow. Our noise wakes up Kit, who turns to look at the strange woman lying beside him. His face registers surprise and fear as he wonders what is happening. A relieved Boon wakes up his wife and takes her back to the guest room. I turn to Kit to reassure him and find Cora laughing her head off. 'You have caught your husband sleeping with another woman in broad daylight!'

No more visitors after that and we are lonely. We miss Sydney, we miss home. It is the three of us in the apartment, we have no kin, we have no friends here. My siblings are all in Kuala Lumpur and I miss them. I have some old friends, but they are also in KL. I talk to Cora about my home town and sisters. She is also a KL person and suggests moving to KL. I consult our second son and he is receptive to the idea. The bright lights of KL, capital of Malaysia, beckon.

Move to Kuala Lumpur

The decision to move to Kuala Lumpur is made. I contact my siblings, who I have yet to see, to inform them. I receive good news from sister Mei. Her daughter, a UK citizen, has a luxury apartment nestled in the KL hills. She and her family visit every year during the English winter, so she will not need the apartment until November. My niece has invited me to stay. Years ago, she, her husband and stepsons had stayed with us in our home in Beecroft, Sydney. She is happy to return the hospitality.

My only disappointment is the husband of another niece. He had always been so kind. I had stayed on more than one occasion at his home. He took me out for food and fun. I looked forward to seeing him. He tells me his father-in-law has come down with dementia and will not be able to help me, misunderstanding my appeal. What I actually need is contacts in KL: a reliable doctor, a dentist, an odd job man. Most of all, I need a good place to stay when November comes, for I will have to rent again. He is the one with the local knowledge. A year later he is back to himself, the most obliging and kind person. Meanwhile, our second son returns to help us move to KL. But first a quick visit to Singapore so we can re-enter Malaysia and renew our visas. We leave Cora to help pack the household items.

We rent an airconditioned minivan, the largest available, to move us and our precious possessions: Kit's electric armchair, the wheelchair, walker and shower chair. I had hoped to squeeze the newly purchased laundry and kitchen items under our seat and between our legs but Cora had different ideas. She generously gave away a number of items for a more comfortable road trip to KL! The receptionist at the office of the apartments received many early Christmas presents that year.

I believe that as a Shanghainese I have good business acumen and money management skills, but somehow I seem to be spending more and more. Yet I cannot economise and compromise, for Kit's well-being and comfort takes priority. Cora's salary is AU$3k a month, and I have to feed her too. Then there are her unexpected dental and medical bills. Rent in Penang was another AU$3k. And so the list goes on. At least there is a break now, as I will not have to pay rent for a while. The one request from my niece is to employ Alice, her young housekeeper. I will also use some of the savings to buy some presents for my sister Mei.

It is a cheerful group that leaves Penang for the next destination. The drive is pleasant, as the British left a good road system, using the local rubber which made the roads the best in south-east Asia. However on the outskirts of KL there is a two hour delay caused by a minor accident between two trucks. It takes a long time for the traffic police to arrive.

We arrive at the exclusive hill district. Housekeeper Alice welcomes us into an expansive and attractive apartment with commanding views. It is actually two apartments, bought separately, but my niece and her husband had knocked out the dividing wall and made some renovations. The original apartment was for her and her husband, the one we were to stay in was for friends and relatives. Down below us is a huge royal palace of the Malaysian King. This apartment block predates the palace. The sun is streaming onto the dark attractive furniture in the large sitting room, giving it a regal air. What is there not to like?

Sister Mei turns up with her husband to welcome us. Brother-in-law has his warm charm and smile and in no time he is chatting with Kit. He sends for a workman to fix Kit's armchair so Kit can watch TV comfortably that evening. He is that sort of person, always concerned for others. It is impossible to be other than happy in this beautiful place.

Our second son spends the night in the room next to us and is gone the next day, back to Sydney. Cora takes over the room.

Kit and I do not live charmed lives, and the unexpected happens. I find Cora in tears the next morning. She tells me she has had a visitation from a ghost and has not slept a wink. She tells me it is a legless female ghost, dressed in black, who keeps gliding between her room and mine. Cora cannot see the face, only the back of the ghost. She feels the ghost is malevolent and will return. Cora shows me the goose pimples on her arms as she talks about it. She swears she will not sleep another night in that room. She will move in with Alice.

Cora is not finished yet. She tells me she is terrified. She believes the ghost will harm her. She says she is sorry but she will only work day hours. If I want her to live in I will have to leave the apartment. She tells me to look for replacement. Kit is used to her and likes her, and I know will be upset. What do I do?

Meanwhile I have already made arrangements to return to Singapore for further treatment on my shoulder. My plan is to stay with good friend Irene for three days. Cora knows of my plans. She gives me three days to work out what to do. She will share a room with Alice and the two of them will look after Kit while I am in Singapore. I will have to pay an extra bonus. Cora is now even more convinced of the ghost, as Alice told her of hearing noises but not seeing anyone. There is the belief that when your luck is down you see a ghost and the ghost chooses by whom they want to be seen. The two girls believe that Cora has been selected. They are not averse to telling me that I might be the next target! The girls are Catholics, but many in Asia, regardless of religion, believe in ghosts.

I take my problems to Irene, who is a staunch Christian. Irene is practical and realistic. She feels that all this is unhealthy. Even if Cora works nine to five or leaves her employment, the apartment is no longer a happy place to stay in. Irene feels that I should leave the apartment as soon as I get back to KL. I feel tired and depressed but I take her advice.

We move to my favourite hotel in Mid Valley. It is in a big shopping complex with a wide choice of cuisine. Cora is overjoyed. Alice is now working for me. Kit and I stay in the hotel while the two girls adjourn to their rented rooms each evening and return each morning. Most migrant workers in KL maintain a rented room.

Brother Kwok's son has learnt of my problems. He comes to the hotel in the morning to take me house hunting. The two girls look after Kit while I am away. We finally find a large apartment that will fit Kit's needs, and we move out of the hotel after ten days. Yes, the sitting room is large and so too the master bedroom. The bathroom is large enough for the shower chair to move in and out. I had assumed that all good sized and expensive apartments had food outlets within walking distance. I make a mistake, this particular one does not. The other problem is I do not inform the landlord early enough that I want the apartment for at least three months. He has taken another deposit and we have to leave at the end of the month.

So again I go house hunting. This time I have some luck. I find a similar apartment some floors below and I snap it up.

Things settle down and life brightens up with a visit from our daughter and eldest granddaughter. We eat out often, as our girls love the Malaysian food. And Kit is happy.

Our last months in Malaysia

Life has not been easy since moving out of my niece's luxury apartment. Alice has become difficult and extravagant with my money. She refers to Kit and me as the "rich Australians". I had to let her go! I now employ a young cook cum cleaner, who prepares our lunch and helps with Kit and his wheelchair.

The search for food turns out to be a problem. It is too exhausting to take Kit out for lunch every day. Our transport is by taxi and we need both our helpers, Cora and the new cook, to move Kit around in his wheelchair. On the other days I am running around by myself to buy cooked food or fresh meat and vegetables for preparation at home.

My hearing is deteriorating, I am nursing a bad shoulder and often exhausted. Kit is having difficulty getting through to me. He is telling Cora how he misses Sydney. He wants to go home. He wants to live at home and cannot understand why he cannot! The sad fact was that living at home is no longer viable. Our small apartment in Sydney is not suitable for a sickly, wheelchair-dependent old man. His wife, at 79 years of age, is not strongly built and of recent years has been subject to bouts of vertigo. Besides Kit is still a tall and well-built man. We are here in Malaysia because wife Li still wants a life together. To spend a few more good years together.

Our three children have had several meetings and decided that Kit will have to go into a nursing home. I feel that, like me, Kit is a free spirit, he cannot be caged. He would rather not live than go into an aged care facility.

Kit had wanted to go home as early as after two months in Penang, but had not said so because he felt that I wanted to stay. Penang had turn out to be boring. The highlights were the visits of the family, planned by me, knowing that Kit would enjoy their visits. Even our youngest son, who was not a keen traveller, had managed a five day visit and his father had been delighted. He had counted the days to all their visits.

Kit passed his days watching TV. He enjoyed action movies. The Bruce Lee movies were his favourites. He watched some of them over and over again. His bedtime was nine at night, but, like a child, he would ask for extensions. I usually agreed to make up for the simple meals he had when everyone was too tired: the simple congee, the soggy Kentucky Fried Chicken and McDonalds.

It was during the boring days that the subject of Genting Highlands came up. It was the landlord of the second apartment who mentioned it when he came to collect the rent in cash. He was a most friendly person and loved chatting. He pointed to the mountains in the distance where, on a clear day, one could make out the resort. Cora had her store of information to add. The casino rooms were cheap and the food good. What won me over were the noodles, dumplings and congee, Kit's favourite food of late. And of course the poker machines! How could I forget? I had been there for one of the VI reunions. At that reunion the schoolmates I knew had not turned up. My luck at the machine had been bad and I had largely forgotten about that trip. Cora was most enthusiastic. She enjoyed a little gamble and had been there several times before. Two days later we were headed for the mountains, Kit and I, Cora and our new help, Muna.

The Genting Highlands Resort was 60 kilometres from KL, a two hour drive along excellent roads. The casino and its hotel were at an elevation of 6,000 feet, 22°C by day and 12°C at night. This was the temperature range that Kit missed. Besides good food and a huge retail outlet, there were theme parks and a modern cable car.

Kit seemed to have lost interest in gambling. He had been a most unusual gambler, as he had good self-control. When he felt his luck was down he would leave regardless of the time. It could still be early and he would drag a protesting Li with him. I played small and never worried about control. Kit would

175

reimburse my losses. He had enjoyed playing Blackjack, but at the Genting Casino he played table games along with Cora and at small stakes. He told me to go to the machines and we would meet back at an appointed time. Kit enjoyed the place and the food, so we had many escapes there.

Trip to Malacca

Our next holiday was to Malacca when our second son flew in again from Sydney. I was relaxed when he was with us, as was he was a keen sportsman and kept himself fit. I had suggested to him that Malacca was an interesting place to visit. I had been there for a day trip as a teenager while he had never been. Malacca was known to be picturesque and had a colourful history, for ships from afar would visit to trade in spices. It was also known for its Peranakan food and low cost of living.

Second son organised the rental of a holiday apartment for five days. The high cost surprised me. I hoped we would get a good holiday. It was to be Kit's last.

From KL we organised an air conditioned minivan, as we had to take the wheelchair and shower chair. We planned a small detour to the town of Kajang, home of the famous Malay satay. This dish consisted of small pieces of marinated meat: chicken, beef or lamb (and intestines for the more sophisticated in taste!) cooked over an open flame. It came with a delicious spicy peanut sauce, accompanied by cucumber, onions and squares of compressed cooked rice. It was a favourite among Malaysians and expatriates, including Kit.

It was one of Kit's good days. He put in an unbelievable performance, eating fifteen skewers of satay! There was no coughing, no choking. No talking either, just pure enjoyment in eating.

The road journey was smooth and we made good time. The apartment was classy, overlooking the Malacca River, explaining why it was pricey!

We spent the next two days sightseeing. With second son's help we went to places we would not have gone otherwise, for he had the strength to manage the wheelchair, even pushing uphill. We searched out places with good Peranakan food.

It was on the second morning that we visited the Portuguese fortress, or rather its remains. This was the famous A'Formosa, built in 1511, brain child of Admiral Alfonso de Albuquerque. He had made the longest journey of a colonial power yet to establish the Portuguese empire in the East.

I made my way to the part of the wall that look out to the sea. It was not difficult to imagine the desperate eyes of the besieged Portuguese soldiers looking out to sea, praying for the arrival of reinforcements. I remember reading how the church bells rang as Portuguese ships were sighted and the siege by the neighbouring hostile powers was lifted yet again. The fortress, with its soldiers, held power for 130 years until they were defeated by the more powerful Dutch forces in 1641.

Nearby was the empty grave of another man of distinction, a Spanish Jesuit missionary who also came across the world, but in this case for his religious beliefs, St Francis Xavier. He had been buried here in Malacca, but later his body was exhumed and enshrined in the Portuguese colony of Goa.

Last, but not least, was my favourite historical character, Admiral Zheng He (Cheng Ho) of the Ming Dynasty of China. He had also set foot on Malacca. I believe he was the greatest maritime personality. His first voyage was officially dated as 1405, but there were Ming Dynasty reports of voyages in 1403. Several years ago I attended a big exhibition on Zheng He Maritime Museum in Hong Kong. The exhibition highlighted his seven voyages to as far as Africa. There were replicas of his armadas and those of the western countries, England, Spain, Portugal, France. Zheng He's sea vessels was shown to be far more advanced than the others.

Zheng He's story was also a most interesting one. He was a Mongolian and a Muslim. As a boy he had been captured in battle and castrated. As a eunuch he had been looked down upon by the Confucian scholars, who gave him little credit and refused to write about his exploits. But Zheng He's enemies were not able to destroy him. He had intelligence and ability. He rose through the ranks of the naval officers to become the most outstanding naval figure in Chinese history.

Some sources reported that during one of Zheng He's voyages he took a Chinese princess as a bride for the local ruler in Malacca. The princess was accompanied by 500 retainers. This was the beginning of the nonyas and babas, a group of Chinese who intermarried with the locals. Their descendants wore the local dress, the sarong and kebaya, ate the local food modified by their diet from China, spoke the local dialect, but identified themselves as ethnically Chinese. The food was to become the Peranakan food, well known in Malacca and Penang, where the nonyas and babas had settled.

The five days in Malacca were very enjoyable. On his morning jogs in the neighbourhood, our second son found hawker stalls. There were his parents' childhood favourites, the Yong tow foo (fish paste stuffed into bean curd), large green and red chillies, and a variety of vegetables. In addition there was a dish seldom sold in KL, but available here: rice cakes fried in egg and chilli oil. Both Kit and I enjoyed the food.

The ride down the Malacca River was most pleasant and possible only with our son's help. The walk along the riverside with me and Cora pushing was enjoyable, too. On the last day I tried to locate the Portuguese village where I had been before, but it was gone and so too the little restaurant where they had served a delicious chicken pie. Instead, we found a big restaurant that sold us contaminated food. Cora suffered the most. It was an uncomfortable journey home with compulsory stops. For the next two days I looked after Kit. Second son and

Kit fortunately ate little of the okra dish and were okay. Then our son left for Sydney.

The last Christmas

Life was lonely again, but our daughter and two granddaughters would be visiting for Christmas. This was all planned before we left Sydney, and I had contributed money to help with the airfares. Our existence seemed to be all highs and lows. Was there some sort of premonition that Kit's journey in life was nearing its end? Each sunset in the apartment seemed to cast a certain sadness. Each night in bed I would rest my head on Kit's shoulder for a few minutes to reassure myself that he was physically there with me. I would listen to the soft breathing as he rapidly fell asleep.

As Christmas approached my spirits lifted. I was surprised to see Kuala Lumpur so lavishly decorated, with Christmas trees, tinsel and lights all over town. As a child growing up in British Malaya I loved the festive season. In those days I saw more English people than I did Malays, for the latter kept to the kampongs in the rural areas. Christmas was welcomed by my family, as it was busy in the shops, a time of increased earnings and happiness.

My memories of the 1950s came tumbling back. Some eight shops away from ours was Nanto's milk bar. One of the girls working there thought I was cute and had invited me in many a time for a free ice cream. But at Christmas time I was warned to stay away, for Nanto's was a favourite of the young British soldiers. I often heard music and laughter coming from there at night.

Could I ever forget the time when brother Kwok ran afoul of the British soldiers? It was nearly Christmas in 1950 when three drunken soldiers attacked him as he unlocked the back door of the shop to come in. Kwok was home from a party, while the soldiers had drifted over from Nanto's. The three drunks had swooped on him. They gave him "the works". Kwok managed to stagger up the stairs to the sitting room, lost consciousness and was found by the housemaids early the next morning. I caught sight of him. His face was badly swollen and his eyes half closed. He complained of pain in his shoulders and his chest, for the soldiers had rained blows down on him. Had he managed to raise the alarm the workers at the dry cleaning shop would have given the soldiers a good workout. There were about eight of them living on the premises.

In 1956 I had two classmates who dated British soldiers and would rave about their blue eyes, long eye lashes and blond hair. As for me, I wanted nothing to do with them!

Back to 2019, excitement built as the day of the arrival of our daughter and granddaughters approached. Meanwhile, I decided to give a party on Christmas night.

My first purchase was a large Christmas tree with tinsel, decorative ornaments and lights. Cora enjoyed decorating the tree and the sitting room. For the next two weeks the coloured lights came on every night, creating a festive atmosphere. In the mornings I was out at the shops, searching for Christmas presents for the party guests, family and friends. I was most happy when I found the almost perfect shirt for Kit. The design was subtle and the colours suited Kit's fair complexion.

The arrival of our granddaughters and daughter gave Kit much happiness. The apartment was filled with laughter as the girls dug into the Malaysian cakes and fruit!

The day of the party came. My siblings and their families arrived. Kit recognised them and called out their names. There was so much warmth as brother Kwok and brother-in-law Keong greeted him. Kwok's son had brought along my younger sister, Chien. Chien loved parties and appreciated being included. Our granddaughters met up with their cousins and caught up on the missing years. Then came the friends. As with Malaysian parties, lots of eating and chatting. The catered Malay food turned out to be very tasty. I had wanted a satay party, but open fires were not allowed in the apartment. Kit was full of smiles. He had always loved company. Everyone commented on how well he looked. The last half hour of the party saw everyone happily occupied with "doggy bagging" the food, as there was so much, and it was so tasty that they were delighted to take some home! Kit and I went to bed exhausted but happy.

There were still a few days left of the three girls' Malaysian holiday. I had booked two days accommodation at the Genting Highland resort for them as well as Kit, Cora and me. It was quality time they were spending with Kit. They took Kit for walks, pushing his wheelchair. They got him into the cable car and had a photograph taken. We ate well, enjoying the different cuisines in the restaurants. Soon the girls were gone.

The year 2019 came to an end. A new year began: 2020.

We had decided to return to Sydney and reassess our situation there. Maybe we would return to Malaysia. We could not continue to live together in our apartment in Sydney. I did not have the physical strength to care for Kit. We did not have the funds to live together in Australia. Kit did not want to spend lonely nights by himself in an aged care home, where I could only visit. I wanted to spend my nights next to him, stretch out my hand to touch him, to kiss his forehead and smooth his white hair!

At this stage I have to comment on the ironies of life. It was in mid-January 2020 that I discovered the ideal apartment that would have given Kit and me what we wanted. Thinking ahead, in case we decided to come back to live, I met up with a housing agent in Mid Valley, my favourite shopping complex, which also had luxury apartments next to it. They were linked by a wide passage, great for wheelchairs. It took less than five minutes to get to the complex, which had over 20 food outlets and restaurants. The supermarkets had fresh produce, seafood and meats. There were walkways and paths to small gardens. It was not expensive to get to the large gardens nearby by taxi. We could have taken Kit there every other day for walks.

I was taken to see a few of the apartments. They were larger and more luxurious, more expensive than the apartments we were staying in, but still affordable. It would have been worth it for the gardens and walks would have given Kit pleasure. The choice of food would have given him more enjoyment. I would be less tired, as I would not have to search for food.

Why were we not told? Why did I not discover these apartments before? Why was Kit not allowed a dream time when he was so near journey's end?

I had wanted so desperately to have a happy time with Kit. To be on Golden Pond, to watch the sunset together holding hands! Was I asking too much? Do I expect too much of life?

I had my final conversation with Cora. Cora had proved to be capable and loyal. Kit appreciated her. She had taken the load off me but I was also realistic enough to know that she had obligations to her family back in the Philippines. I paid for her return fare home. I gave her everything we bought for our apartment, taking only personal items. Cora sent a trunk back to her mother containing much that we had given her. I told her we would let her know if decide to return to Malaysia again. She told us that she preferred to work for us. In the meantime, she was going to have a long holiday at home with her mother and son.

The Last Chinese New Year

We stay for Chinese New Year. The last one we had celebrated was 42 years ago. I want Kit to enjoy the festive foodstuffs. He prefers the savoury titbits while I enjoy the sweet items. Little Li has loved the candied sweet meats since discovering them at the age of four on the ancestors' worship table on the eve of New Year in 1944. Chinese New Year in 2020 was on 25 January.

Sister Meng, as the eldest Zhang daughter, hosts the family reunion at her house. It is a playback to the days when our parents were alive. The difference is that we are now the seniors, the older generation. We give the lucky money, the ang pows, to the young ones, the grandchildren and the housemaids. I take Cora and the new maid to the lunch. Meng's preparations are simple. There are no elaborate decorations, unlike our childhood days, but there is good food. It is the people who are important. Brother Kwok is there with his son and daughter. His presence is important, for he is the eldest and all the siblings are still alive. Brother Yeh is in an aged care home in Melbourne and is in touch with us. I visit him every year. We were not taught to be demonstrative, never touching or hugging, but the love lives strongly in our hearts.

Younger sister Chien is the cook. There are our mother's traditional Shanghainese dishes; Shanghainese white rice slices fried with wong bak, pork and mushrooms, Shanghainese spring rolls. I reproduced these two dishes for my children in Australia every year. My mother's famous dessert, glutinous rice with eight treasures, is missing as it is an elaborate dish that takes too much time and is much too sweet. She never knew that I could make that dish! We also have the traditional jellyfish dish, except that Chien forgot to soak it over night to get rid of the salt.

Kit is happy and makes small talk with everyone. Meng is Kit's favourite sister-in-law, as he finds her kind and gentle. I have dressed Kit in a new red Chinese shirt with Chinese collar and buttons. He looks bright, chirpy and happy. It is his last Chinese New Year. It is to be brother Kwok's last Chinese New Year, too.

There are things missing at Meng's place, things that live in my memory which cannot be erased. Every year in the shophouse there were the familiar decorations. In the corner, standing tall, were two stalks of sugar cane. I think their presence was to bring cleanliness and sweetness to the household. Then there were the tall vases, the tallest one with the pussy willows and the shorter one filled with gladioli of white and orange. Pasted on the walls were red paper cut-outs of the Chinese characters Luck and Longevity. These paper cuttings were sold in the market weeks before New Year's Day. But Meng and her children are Christians, while our days in the past were those of Buddhists. It was the housekeeper, Ah Heng Char, who did all the decorations. Those days were in the 1940s, days long gone …

Return to Sydney: The long journey home

It had been a long lunch at sister Meng's. We returned to the apartment and had an early night. The next day, 26 January, was a quiet one, with Kit watching movies on TV as I did the final packing and checked that all our bills had been settled. Our second son flew in and there was a sigh of relief from me.

We were all up early on January 27. Cora gave Kit an early morning shower, for it was going to be a long day for him. Cora would stay another three days in the apartment and clean up the place. Kit was deeply appreciative of the care that she gave him. He had a little over five hundred Malaysian dollars on him, half of it the winnings from our last visit to the casino at Genting. He handed Cora half of the total, a gift for last minute shopping before she returned to Manila. It was a gesture from him, as he knew that I had given her a big cash present besides her flight tickets. Since I took over the finances Kit never handled large sums of money. He never asked for cash, but I would hand him small amounts regularly. If he had more he would have given her more. Cora also appreciated the kindness of this Chinese gentleman who had the misfortune to be crippled and to suffer poor health.

It was a sad goodbye to Cora, our companion and helper for nine months. We did not know whether we would see her again.

The flight back to Sydney was stressful and tiring for all three of us. I had failed to realise how sick Kit had become. When we left Sydney he could take a few steps, now he could not. He had deteriorated. The long hours on the plane confused him. He attempted to urinate three times unsuccessfully. As business class passengers we were given the use of an enclosed area where we could change his diapers.

184

Our son had to carry him. Kit could not sleep. We finally reached Sydney by nightfall. We were all exhausted.

We had organised a number of things ahead of our arrival. Our taxi man, Charlie, met us at the airport. Charlie helped to get Kit in and out of the taxi. We got Kit back to our apartment. I could see the fatigue on our son's face. He was close to falling over. We managed to get Kit onto his bed and to finally lie down ourselves.

We did not know that this was to be Kit's last night at home, the apartment we had moved into in 2011.

As planned with our daughter's help, the next morning we moved Kit into the aged care home, some ten minutes away, as a temporary arrangement. We had planned to bring him home and go on holidays with the children. On 1 February we collected Kit from the aged care home for our Chinese New Year family reunion dinner, which we had at a good Chinese restaurant not too far away. It was to be our last family dinner.

February slowly passes. We have not finalised our plans. Kit is unhappy in the aged care home. He had stayed there before and found it pleasant. The previous general manager, an efficient and capable person, who was also warm and friendly, has retired and the place has changed. Getting into this home in the past had been difficult. I was surprised when my daughter told me she had no difficulty booking when we were still in KL. Kit had always been given an upstairs room when he was there for respite care, now he is in a downstairs room. What is most upsetting are three dementia patients in his ward. Kit finds he is often awakened by their screams. Things come to a head on 22 February, when the most disturbed of the dementia patients breaks into his room. She stands at the bottom of his bed, screaming. He presses the alarm bell but it is a long time before someone comes to take her away!

Kit expresses his unhappiness to his son and daughter and we discuss what we should do to alleviate his distress. A few days later I experience one of the most upsetting nights in my life.

A storm is brewing as the sun goes down. There is lighting and thunder, rain pours down. It is a rare wild night. The phone rings. It must be around two o'clock in the morning – an SOS call from Kit. A call I shall never forget. He begs me to let him come home. His pleas tear into me. I wonder whether I should drive over, but the storm is raging on, the lightning keeps flashing. I am confused and frightened. What do I do? I want to hold him and comfort him. Can I manage to get to him through the storm at this hour? I try to be realistic. I tell him I will be there early in the morning, that he will be well looked after by the carers and not to worry. I feel such a coward. I stay at home.

I recall that night subsequently with so much pain. In hindsight I realise that Kit must have been desperate to have persuaded the night nurse to allow him to make the call. He had always been a most reasonable man, never one to make demands. I should have gone to him. I console myself that I would have gone had it not been storming. It was the second saddest night in my life, the saddest night being the night he left this world little more than a fortnight later.

The next morning I am at the aged care home. I rush to his room but it is empty. The wild storm has caused leaking to that wing and the patients have been moved. I run to him as his bed is wheeled out together with the others. He looks tired and subdued. I think the awful night has taken the fight out of him.

On 27 February, our second son, daughter and I have a meeting with the General Manager and the head nurse. The request to transfer Kit to an upstairs room is rejected. Kit is crestfallen but he does not complain anymore.

Kit's swallowing problems return. He is put on a purée diet. He does not enjoy his food. Our daughter brings in some tasty snacks, which we cut into small bits and feed to him. We can see that he can still enjoy flavoursome food.

On the morning of 29 February Kit was found on the floor next to his bed. No one knows how long he had been lying there I am told when I come in. They tell me they had tried to contact me earlier that morning. They say he must have jumped out from the bed. I say he could not have done that with the beds restraining bars in place. They tell me that the person who put him to bed must have forgotten to pull up the bars!

There is more bad news: the fall from the bed has caused the collapse of one of his lungs. I find him seated at breakfast. He looks alright, but is very subdued. I inform the children of what has happened to Kit. The nurse tells me they are keeping an eye on him and they reassure me they will do what is necessary. My family and I are concerned about Kit. There has been gross neglect, but we are not looking to blame.

There are no complaints from Kit, so we do not know whether he is in pain. However, on the next day he is unwell and remains in bed. An assessor arrives from Concord Hospital and she decides to move him to the hospital. It is Monday, 2 March 2020.

Transfer to Concord Hospital

February seems to have passed with me in a daze. I keep notes and try to write of the developments each evening. I do not know whether I realised how critical things were for Kit. I only remember my feelings of not wanting or believing that Kit would leave me, that his journey was ending, that I would have to carry on by myself.

Tuesday, 3 March, and Kit is moved to the geriatrics ward. He appears tired and listless, eating little and eyes often closed. The next day he is moved to Intensive Care for oxygen and intravenous feeding. Then he is back in the geriatrics ward.

Meanwhile, our daughter has found another aged care home for him, Redleaf Manor, one that cost a lot more but gave better care. At this stage I did not care if we used up all our savings!

187

While in Intensive Care Kit had spoken to the doctors. He expressed his wish for his life to end. He did not want it prolonged by intravenous feeding, or to be linked up with machines that would breathe for him and keep him alive. He instructed them to let him leave this life. And please not let his wife know!

By 6 March, Kit is in a comfortable room at Redleaf and I have found my niche in the bay window that looks out to the car park and part of the grounds. Kit and the family are happier in this sunlit room. Kit has developed breathing problems because of the collapsed lung and needs oxygen. News has gone out that Kit is unwell and dear, close friends start to visit. On 7 March Kit complains of continuous pain and is given morphine. More friends arrive. Kit makes an effort to greet them, for he appreciates their visits. I am with him until nightfall, then I go home to shower and go to bed. Home is only 20 minutes away.

On Sunday, 8 March I get an early morning call from Redleaf that Kit has been taken to Concord Hospital, as he is incontinent. I find him there. It was expected that he would be sent back to Redleaf but they decide to keep him. The hospital authorities give me permission to stay and I move into the hospital room with him. All they say is that he is a very sick man. I am given a small low bed at the corner of his room. I am grateful. I am able to see him each time I wake during the night.

Dear friend Lillian flies in from Melbourne with her daughter. Her husband was one of Kit's best friends. Old friendships run deep and she is here for two days. Kit has many such friends.

Monday, 9 March the geriatrician informs us that Kit might not last until tomorrow. I cannot sleep, and spend the hours watching him. Kit makes it through the night.

The next day he is drowsy. They decide to put the oxygen mask on him. The family is there in the morning. Our second son and youngest son are by his side most of the time. Our daughter never fails to turn up each day. One of them brings me lunch. I get a bread roll from the hospital cafeteria for dinner. I sleep on my little bed in the corner of Kit's hospital room for another night. The next day, 11 March, at 5:00 pm the hospital ambulance sends Kit back to Redleaf. I ride back with him.

A journey ends

We are back at Redleaf. I sleep on a thin mattress on the floor of Kit's room. The children bring me fresh clothes and food. I shower in the attached bathroom, I do not need to leave the room. When night time comes Kit is surrounded by his two younger sons, daughter and two granddaughters.

On 12 March the loved ones are here again. I enjoy the takeaway dinner they have brought. We know that Kit would have loved to join us in eating if he could. He returns the love by giving weak smiles whenever he can.

I will always remember that night, for I received one of the sweetest, yet most painful, memories in my life. After the children had gone and there were only the two of us in the room, Kit opened his eyes wide. They rested on me and he gave me his beautiful deep smile. He had this special smile which I loved. It was his goodbye smile. His eyes lingered on me for a few moments before they closed. He seemed to have drifted off again. By this time he was having four-hourly morphine injections for his pain.

I recall Kit telling me several times through the years that he had no regrets in life. He also told me that he never regretted marrying me.

Throughout the last week Kit does not talk, but he has found a way to show his love. I often rest my hand over his. Then I slip my fingers into his cupped hand. I find that he responds by returning the pressure. He is too weak to do more than that. He responded likewise when our daughter pressed his hand. To our sons and granddaughters he would give a weak smile. I felt I could sense his feelings the last few nights. He wanted to go, as he could see we were suffering too. Yet he could feel the love around him and he also wanted to stay with us. This struggle was hurting him. He was holding on through sheer willpower, for he'd had no nourishment for days. I think it was on the night of 12 March that I whispered to him 'Go Kit, go in peace. Do not worry about us.'

On 13 March Kit struggles to breathe. He gets his morphine injection and drifts off to sleep. Mid-morning and we have visitors. Our accountant, who is also a friend, turns up to go through our accounts for submission to the ATO. Our other visitors stand around sadly looking at Kit. They are medical colleagues who know that these are his last days. From time to time Kit opens his eyes and gives a weak smile. He does not talk, the effort is too much.

At night the children come with food for dinner. The two sons are there, our daughter, two granddaughters and the younger granddaughter's boyfriend who visited us in Penang. Then everyone is gone again and Kit and I are alone.

His eyes are closed. He seems very tired. I return to my thin uncomfortable mattress next to the bay window and lie down. I have thoughts of climbing into his bed, but Kit is lying right in the middle and there is not enough space on either side for me.

As usual, I only doze. Every time I awaken I check to see that he is breathing. Then at 12:35 am a nurse comes in. I jump up because I suddenly feel cold. She checks his breath. He is gone! When? She tells me they last checked twenty minutes ago. His body is still warm. Dear God, I wanted to hold him for the last time before his last breath. He looks like he's still asleep. He looks serene and at peace. He is no longer in pain. Kit's journey has ended ...

The funeral

Our daughter is the first to be informed of her father's passing. I sit in the small room outside Kit's room, waiting for my daughter to turn up. The nurse and another helper are dressing Kit's body. I am in a daze. The only thought going through me is 'He is gone, he is gone!'

She arrives. She is in pain too. She arranges for the funeral directors to take Kit away to prepare his body for the funeral. They tell us that they need two days. I am drowsy and doze fitfully, but I know he is gone and it is not a dream. The two days pass.

Our eldest son is back from Queensland. The other children had wanted him back earlier, so there is no big welcome for him. I am happy he is here. I want no blame. I can see the pain on his face; he did love his father. Who knows how much damage the Church of Scientology did to him? Who knows the pain he went through, his mental struggles? I want him to know that his father loved him and that he still has a mother who loves him. What is important is that the four children are back together. It is a time for remembrance of their father and a time for love.

We are all at the funeral parlour and allowed to see Kit. With all the embalming fluids Kit looked a waxwork figure, but we can see a calm and peaceful look on his face. No more pain. I slip my finger into his folded hands, almost expecting some pressure back! In my mind and in my heart I speak to him. I tell him that we loved him always and know that he loved us. That we know, wherever he has gone, he will do whatever he can do for us. Then each of the children go up to spend some silent moments with him and say their final farewells.

It was COVID-19 time in March 2020. Many did not turn up at the funeral, but it was a warm group of close friends that greeted me as the hearse drove in. It was my last ride with Kit as we drove to where the service was held. I could only tell him that it would not be long before I will join him.

The funeral was dignified and solemn. We played his favourite tunes and showed slides and photos of his life. It was a celebration of his life. The speeches were short, made by his friends and children. It was a time of love. We behaved as he would have wanted. Just silent sorrow, no outward and public display of grief. The service ended with family and friends viewing and inwardly saying a final farewell to Kit.

We adjourned to a nearby room for drinks and the appetising food we had ordered. Kit would have wanted everyone to have a good feed. There were friends we had not seen for a while. We chatted with them, talked of happier times, and thanked them for coming. We did what Kit, the Confucian gentleman, would have wanted of us.

Li's Confucian Gentleman

Grief

It took 15 months of deep sadness before I could return to the life still before me. No, it was not too long, considering the time Kit and I had been together – 62 years since I was 17. During those 15 months my heart was so heavy with pain. Not only was there grief and pain, there was also unhappiness, bitterness and regret. I wished to go rather than journey along alone.

I decided to find relief in writing. The words came pouring out like water from a broken dam. My first memoir, *The Reluctant Migrant's Daughter*, was born. It was cathartic, it brought me solace, removing the load that lodged within me. Slowly, I came to understand that Kit had freed me. I was free to move on.

Epilogue

It has been a long journey, one of discovery, of ups and downs, of joys and sorrows. I remember myself best as the five year old child happily skipping between the two shops. At times I would be sitting on the steps of the staircase, or standing in an obscure corner observing the workers. I was always careful not to get into anybody's way. I did not want to be the cause of any trouble.

True, I was a neglected child, often by myself and lonely. Yet I discovered freedom. I was not watched or followed. I could go wherever I wanted. No one made demands of me. I wanted no conflict, but as a young adult I encountered it when I met Grace.

I learnt anger, bitterness and pain. I had little understanding of life. My journey has been long, but I did learn. I learnt that we have an allotted time in this world and we should make good use of it. I found that the average person has no power over life, and does not know what lies before them. I found that life can be a misery. Yet there is also so much beauty around me. It has taken me a long time to learn. The more I learn, the more I find there is to learn.

At the age of 82 I decide to visit the Red Centre of Australia, to see Uluru, enjoy the beauty of the desert night and to experience the spirituality spoken of. I want to know what it is like. The same curiosity, the wanting to know, had taken me to Harbin, China in 1993.

With much excitement I sign up for the expensive "Sounds of Silence" dinner under the stars. The night in the desert reaffirms what I have learnt about life.

The program included watching the sunset over Uluru. As the rays of the setting sun strike the mass that is Uluru it glows a bright burnished red. All too soon it turns brown as the sky darkens. The moon is out long before the stars. The moon is not large, but its light brightens the area.

The group is told to move to the nearby area where tables are set for dinner. In the dying light from the setting sun the digeridoo player moves from table to table, playing his instrument. He is talented, producing a lighter melody than the usual heavier notes. The haunting tune floats into the night air and lingers for a little while.

I want to enjoy the silence of the night, immerse myself in nature. I want silent contemplation. Shrill laughter splits the night air. There is much noise, much talking and laughing. There are some 60 people out there, the young and the old, mostly older people. There are those who want wine and laughter, enjoyment of the night with their partners and friends, merry making.

What one wants may not be the same as what others want. But I am happy that I have received my enjoyment. Other people do matter. Sometimes one's wants may encroach on the happiness of others. Who decides? We should be aware that pain is sometimes inflicted. Is it done blatantly? Is it necessary. There is enough pain in this world of ours. There are natural calamities, diseases beyond our control. Do we need to add more pain? Do we need war? Can man ever learn?

I knows I am but a small player in a corner of the Earth. Perhaps, perhaps, I can help others who have known pain. I do not want a repeat of my pain. I have paid my debts. My journey will end soon. I am ready to face what lies ahead, whether there is another life, whether there is God's world of love or oblivion beyond this life.

It is June 2023. I turn 83 this very month. I enjoy my morning walk; the brightening of the morning sky, the ducks on the water, the galahs pecking the grass seeds on the golf course. I suck in the cold winter air. I am at peace. I enjoy my freedom. I have been fortunate. My journey has been long, but also meaningful. I have learnt to love myself; to know my worth, for I have love and compassion. No longer the spritely five year old, but the older person moving along slowly, cautiously, but still true to the spirit of the child who wanted no conflict, only love. I am myself. I have not been remade. I move serenely towards journey's end.

I will leave this world with a clean slate, a *tabula rasa*. I have fulfilled my obligations. I have paid my debts. I have peace in my mind and in my heart. I do not have to be afraid anymore. I am truly free …

Postscript

Life is unpredictable! How often have I used these words in my memoirs and in my yet to be published novel, *The Eunuch Warrior*? It comes back to me only too brutally on the night of Tuesday, 31 October 2023.

Over the previous fortnight I had felt an unusual mild pain on my right side, below my armpit. I had resumed exercising with light weights. I was eating too much, gorging on Australian fruits, and I needed to lose a few kilos. I had been probably too rigorous in the exercising, and might have strained a ligament.

The pain seemed a bit stronger that Tuesday night. I stopped what I was doing and traced the pain to where I felt was the source. It was coming from my right breast. I carefully examined myself and found a lump. I knew what it was. Breast cancer.

The next morning I saw my general practitioner and told her. She could not find the lump so I guided her to where it was. She made an appointment with a breast surgeon for me, comforting me that we do not know for sure. But I knew.

Three years had passed since Kit went. I had become used to being by myself. I had started to appreciate the beauty around me again. The early morning walks, the soft breeze, the light rain on my face, the song of birds. I was travelling again. To visit brother Yeh in Brisbane and friends in Melbourne. As I felt I was getting on, and not as strong as before, my second son accompanied me to visit sister Meng in Malaysia. In writing my memoirs I felt I had learned to understand life better and to accept what I did not before, to be thankful for my blessings. I had passed my "date due". I was ready to go, but I wanted to go without pain. I had seen how Kit had suffered during the last five years of his life. In February 2023 I had a mini stroke, but suffered no ill effects, no pain or distress.

Again I am reminded that we do not have a choice. Yet I ask WHY? Why must I go in pain? Why can I not close my eyes and just go in my sleep! I am at peace, I am ready. Why am I not allowed to go? I had a full body scan and more bad news. It is a trifecta! I have breast cancer, a tumour in my left cheek and I need to have a colonoscopy to identify another possible cancer.

Why is it that when you wish for little pain there must be more! The biopsies of my breasts prove to be painful, although I was told they would not be. The side effects from the chemotherapy made me ask why I had not died a year ago. Is life that precious?

The appointments are unending: radiologist, oncologist, neurologist, breast surgeon, head and neck surgeon, cardiologist. Yet these are dedicated people who toil away at keeping others alive. Here in Australia the medical standards are high and the practitioners are clearly dedicated. I feel so ungrateful, for they strive to keep me alive when I feel I do not want to battle on.

And so it is one day at a time. It is nearly the end of February 2024 and my surgery is next week, the long haul has only started.

I am reminded that we live in a world where life and death is not ours to decide. So let us go lightly, appreciating the beauty and the good around us. And most of all, the love that surrounds us.

Yet learning does not end until the day you finally go! I am back from my fourth visit to the cardiologist in two months. Each time I have travelled by taxi on my own. I feel I should help myself when I can and not bother others, as the clinic is not far away. I am given the "all clear". I am fit for the forthcoming surgery. I am home on my favourite armchair and my mobile phone rings. It is a call from Singapore, from my dear friends Irene and Amy. They have finally caught me, for I am very deaf and seldom answer calls. They are very concerned, for they know I have cancer. They both talk to me. I assure them I am fine.

I put down my phone and weep.

I got to know Irene well only in later years. She was Kit's classmate, as was her husband, a very close friend of Kit's. I stay with her each time I visit Singapore. She is a gem of a person. As for Amy, I refer to her as my best friend. We met while in university. It has been a long and lasting friendship. She stood by me as I went through the difficult times when I had to miss so many lectures in my final year because of morning sickness. She lent me her notes for those lectures. She shared with me whatever she had on the subjects we did together. Here is a friend I will treasure forever and a day.

Amy reminded me of my good friend Dawn from library school in Melbourne. Dawn would stay back in the library to do the recommended reading while I rushed home to my three young children. She would let me read her findings. I have no doubt I would have passed but perhaps be less knowledgeable. I also had a Girl Friday, Ah Yoke, who helped me look after my children during the years I spent in Melbourne. Currently I have caring friends in Sydney who bring me food. Then I have my editor who helps me with my books. I have only known her two short years, but she is also there in my hour of need. She has given me the support I need. She takes me to the important appointments and provides me with emotional support, so I break out in laughter instead of tears!

Years ago, when I was 14, a kindly Indian man, an acquaintance of my father, read my palm. His words still ring true today. He told me not to expect help, financial or emotional, from my parents, but that I will receive help throughout my life from strangers, from people I will meet as I travel on life's long journey. All this has made me realise that I have lived a very rich life. My friends have added so much colour, given me so much warmth and comfort. My final conclusion is that I am a very lucky person, for I have received so much in this life.

I am very thankful!

Glossary of selected characters

Papa, the Patriarch: Zhang Yu

I adored him as a child. He was the pillar of the Zhang family. I was repeatedly told that I lived well because of him. He was the one responsible for the good life and the plentiful food we always had. Even during the hard times of the Japanese occupation he risked his life to feed us. He was always busy, always working.

He had little time for the children, but sister Meng was his favourite. It annoyed MahMah to see him spend a little of his time with her. Our lives depended on him. Life would have been different for the Zhang children had he lived even a few years longer.

He was still in his prime when he went. He was well respected and loved by the Chinese community in Kuala Lumpur.

MahMah, the Matriarch: Foong Ying

MahMah was hard to fathom. She was tough and outspoken, fearing no one except, perhaps, her husband. She was self-righteous with a strong self-image. She was an intelligent woman.

MahMah was infertile, had no love for children and was harsh to the Zhang siblings, except brother Kwok. She felt that harsh discipline and regular caning was the way to make us stay on "the straight and narrow". She would hurl insults at us, ridicule and tell us we were dirt! But I did see that she had love for a selected few: her husband, some for my brother Kwok and she doted on Weng, the first born of Zhang Yu and Ah Chieh. I learnt ridicule and fear from her, but she did show some concern for the young teenager Li on occasion. It was sad that opium addiction destroyed any ability she had to run the family business. She lost interest. The opium craving dominated her.

Ah Chieh

Ah Chieh was the first person I loved, for she allowed me to love her. She did not have much time for me after she had her own children, but it was enough. I thrived on the crumbs from her table! I learnt love from her and love saw me through life. I have already written much about her.

Ah Heng Char

Ah Heng Char was a baby amah turned housekeeper. She caused me and my siblings much misery. She did not know that our grandfather had put much-needed funds into the family business. She viciously called us parasites and freeloaders. She felt we were siphoning money from the business to be fed. Funds that rightly belonged to Weng, for his father, Zhang Yu, had established a successful business from his hard work. But what sort of life did she have?

She made the journey to Kuala Lumpur from Canton, China when she was barely twenty. What made her join the sisterhood of spinsters, to forsake marriage and family to work as a domestic employee in a foreign land? She had some basic education, for she could read newspapers and often consulted the Chinese almanac for information. It was from her that I first heard about Confucius, the Chinese sage. From her I learnt something about Chinese history, that an imperial family ruled China, that there had been a powerful empress called Cixi.

I remember the few occasions she took me with her to the temple to pray and I had held the joss sticks for her. Ah Heng taught me about the goddess of mercy, Kwan Yin. I knew she had family, for she had also taken me to the Chinese professional letter writers. She had her communication with her family through them. (In the late 1940s there were little booths where writers hawked their business in Chinatown. Uneducated migrants were able to keep in touch with their families through these professional letter writers. The charges were moderate and they provided some happiness for many migrants who still had loved ones back in China.) She also remitted money back to China, as did the many migrants in Malaya.

Ah Heng was frequently cynical and sarcastic. Sister Meng was often her target. She openly showed that she did not like brother Yeh. At one stage her nickname for me was "little worm". I had accepted it without protest, for someone had given me attention!

I remember, too, the occasions I when received some kindness from her. Once, was when I was about ten, I had climbed onto a chair and successfully reached a tin of expensive dates meant for cooking. Only two or three were needed in soups to enhance the flavour. The tin had been full and I ate half of them. Ah Heng did not report me to MahMah. And when I played with little Weng she would often reward me with cookies.

Ah Heng's one great love was Weng, the child she looked after from his birth. In later years, when the family business went downhill, she used her salary to supplement Weng's school needs. But she hurt brother Yeh, for she instigated his caning. It was uncalled for, as Yeh never hurt anyone. Yet I have gratitude towards her, for she was my first history teacher and fed information to the curious child who wanted to know!

Zhang Jen, my father

He hurt me but I must be fair to him. Apart from his good looks, he received few gifts in life. My mother as his wife was perhaps his greatest gift.

Jen was of average intelligence. He was not interested in learning and had no ambitions, neither for himself nor for his children. Neither had he the diplomacy, cunning, or ability to work tirelessly to succeed. Zhang Yu was the only one he was keen to learn from. Zhang Yu was his hero, an older brother who would guide him. He was the faithful follower. Ah Chieh told me that my father was the one who wept most bitterly at Zhang Yu's funeral.

Zhang Jen was content with a simple life. Perhaps he was happiest when he ran the small drycleaning business in Singapore. He earned enough to support himself and my mother and the three children they kept with them, Mei, Sang and Chien. He would never speak out against his cousin, MahMah. She was his revered elder. His ideas were ancient, like those back in China. As a father he thought not of what he owed his children, but what they owed him. He had given them the gift of life. In return he expected unfailing filial piety.

Luk May, my mother

Luk Mei was more realistic, more intelligent and more capable than her husband. In later life she lost a leg in a traumatic bus accident, but she was stoic and accepting of life's cruel blows. In her old age she tried to explain something of her life to sister Meng. She had never been encouraged to think for herself. She was a naive teenager of sixteen when her family married her off. Her marriage had been arranged and her first meeting with my father was on her wedding day!

She told Meng to apologise to her other children for her flaws, for her inability to care for them. She was strictly advised by her parents that she had to be obedient to her husband and to be always there for him. She was a wonderful wife. She never questioned her husband. She accepted all his decisions even when she knew he was wrong. She also told Meng that she was so naive that she thought that, after Zhang Yu died, those of us left at the shop still lived well, that there was plentiful food and housemaids to care for us. But there was nothing she could have done had she known of the emotional and physical abuse to which we were subjected.

Songs of Bereavement

I remember ...

The hours have dragged by

They turn to days

The days to weeks and then months.

It is six months now

Thankfully time has passed,

But love remains.

It cannot have faded into nothingness.

Love sustains me

And maintains me.

I cannot end my life I am told,

So I must travel on

'Till we meet again, my love.

Where are you?

The question has been there
Since you left.
Perhaps the same question
Since life began.
It seemed only yesterday
When we said
'Till death us do part.'
Sad thoughts, painful, heart breaking,
When will the pain end?
Can I come to where you are?
Is there place for me?
God offers me hope,
That there is a tomorrow.
Ten months have passed,
But I remain the same...

Here am I

Here am I,

But you have gone!

Everything is still the same, the bed, the room.

Your armchair is in its usual place

But I sit in it now.

Outside the bedroom, at the far corner

Where the sun shines each morning,

Lie your ashes in your urn,

A beautiful porcelain vase

You brought home many years ago.

You never thought your remains would rest there.

The urn sits behind the photo

Of a smiling middle aged man.

A sprig of orchids bends protectively over the photo.

Near it, a watch you wore each day.

Next, a small bell, used for summoning me to you
in your wheelchair.

Finally a pair of small vases,

You brought home from your first holiday abroad

62 years ago.

Yes, I am here and so is everything

Except you are no longer here.

Special Moments

Special moments, locked in time.

Were you able to lock yours?

At recall, you travel back to the past.

Back to the wedding day.

Three score years ago.

To the happiness

And thoughts of a life together.

All frozen in time.

There were other happy times

But this stands out best

Because I locked it in,

The special moment of my life.

A Journey's End

We were both making this journey.

We were rounding the bend,

Proceeding towards what was once a distant shore.

I dozed off.

The angels came and took you ashore,

Your time had come, you had to go.

You would not have left me voluntarily,

You told me you would never leave me,

I wanted us to leave together.

Alone I drift on

With memories so beautiful

That tears seep down unceasingly.

You are gone and I must continue alone.

Yet as I look up,

I see the beauty around me.

The sunshine, the flowers, the trees,

The gentle breeze that caresses my face

And dries my tears.

So I await my time,

For I know

I will see you waiting for me

At my journey's end …

The Bench

Yes, I am at the bench again,

Seated beside the river.

I am here to talk to my departed love

And to watch the sunset.

Sometimes you control the tears,

Other times unrestrained they flow.

I watch the colours of the sunset,

The birds and the ripples on the water,

Looking for a message.

I tell myself to be practical

Yet I cannot stop the yearning,

The warm smile, the gentle touch.

It is all in the past but it lives in the memories

And so my grief continues.

To the bench I return today,

As I will the next, another sunset,

Always to tell you,

I will always miss you.

The bench (far right) beside Parramatta River

Sadness and Happiness

Poets have tried to describe both,

They are part of our human lives.

Sadness never leaves you.

Not when a loved one departs.

Happiness is fleeting,

Hard to savour, to hold on to.

Enveloped in it,

You are too dazed to realise it is short lived.

It is bittersweet,

Leaving greater sadness ...

Together

I walk along the foreshore,

My thoughts turn to you again.

It is a year now.

My yearnings have never ceased

I no longer seek,

The bright lights, the excitement or the laughter

But simply, I wish

To hold your hand

To sit with you

To touch your face

To lean against you

And feel the warmth and the love.

To recall the years together

Our tears, our fears.

The times of laughter.

The tender moments

The special times.

To rise above the pain

To recall what was beautiful

To sustain me

For the rest of the years

Without you,

Till we meet again ...

Ode to Ashes

They say 'Till death us do part.'

No, we do not!

You will always remain part of me.

Your ashes are what is left

Of your earthly life.

No slow decay,

No sleeping on the cold earth.

You chose to be your ashes

Your remains lie in the urn.

They are with me,

Together with a lifetime of memories.

Memories haunt,

Memories taunt,

To the love that was, is, and will always be,

In this lifetime.

A Song for the Aged

Our loved ones are gone

And we have grown old.

We have lost our looks

And our agility

Yet we still feel and we still love.

Our memories remain, so too our pain.

Do we no longer matter?

Should we be confined to life's junk pile?

My loved ones are gone

But I await my time.

Was it so long ago

That I used to hold the little ones?

Swing them and hear them giggle.

I would place their little feet on mine

And dance them round the room,

Catch them before they fall.

And now they hold my arm,

To stop me from falling.

Youth and strength, age and weakness,

The cycle of life continues.

But love lives on

For we never stop loving.

Acknowledgements

Again to my editor and good friend since beginning my first book. I knew you not until less than two years ago. You are a gem of a person. Without you I do not honestly know whether these two books would have been written!

I have dedicated this second memoir to my sister Meng, who provided me with the encouragement to write it. I felt that I had to bring out everything and she gave me the strength to do it. She was proud of me for writing *The Reluctant Migrant's Daughter*, and that meant a lot to me. It reassured me that our childhood was no made-up story, no fairy tale, but what actually happened.

I have found myself. The migrants around me I recall with tenderness and I am glad they were part of my early life. I can no longer skip around like little Li. I walk proudly, but slowly, with my head held high. I have had a meaningful journey.

Editor's Note

First things first: As I write in late July 2024, Li is cancer-free, the keyhole surgery on her right breast having been successful. No evidence of any spreading cancer cells was found by the surgeon, but, as Li notes in these memoirs, the medicos are zealous and continue to treat her to ensure there is no reoccurrence. The possibly problematic tumour in her cheek and potential issue in her colon are challenges that still lie ahead.

Li is a great survivor. Her innate will to live, intelligence and wicked sense of humour are more than a match for any setback that besets her. Yes, she has and does let others take advantage of her kindness, generosity and sometimes naïve faith in humankind. Yes, she might get depressed after being let down – even by her own body. Still, that curious little five year old child re-emerges time and time again. And the urge to learn, teach and create is a powerful force in Li. Hence these two volumes of memoirs and maybe a couple of novels.

Meanwhile, I recently had the very good fortune to accompany Li and her second son for a couple of weeks in China, Malaysia and Singapore.

Amongst other adventures, we spent some very enjoyable hours with members of Li's family and friends. People who are part of the memoirs I have spent many hours discussing with Li and editing. Li had already brought them to life for me, but here were some of them in person! Luckily for me, good food was as much a priority for them as it has always been for Li.

The photo below shows Li and me next to the river at the Bund in Shanghai. The second photo shows us as Li fulfills a desire to drink a Singapore Sling and throw peanut shells on the floor at the Raffles Hotel in Singapore.

Li and me, June 2024

There is much for which I am grateful to Li. Her friendship, trust, humour and tolerance. Her fascinating stories, only a fraction of which made it into her memoirs. The delicious fruit and jellies she almost force-fed me to keep me coming back, week after week, to listen and talk through her nearly perfect draft chapters. Her understanding of my coffee habit. Her generosity and indomitable spirit.

We should be glad there are people like Li in our lives. Role models such as she are rare and to be treasured.

DC

Credits

Page 17: Li's family tree design thanks to Family Tree Builder, copyright © 2023 MyHeritage Ltd

Page 25: Photo of the chamber pot, by Unknown Author, is licensed under CC BY-SA-NC

Page 32: Photo of the durian is thanks to مانفى CC BY-SA 4.0 <https://creativecommons.org/licenses/by-sa/4.0>, via Wikimedia Commons, https://commons.wikimedia.org/wiki/File:Durian_in_black.jpg

Page 27: Photos of the BB Dance Hall next to the main entrance to the BB Park and Lucky World thanks to https://www.skyscrapercity.com/threads/kuala-lumpur-old-pictorial-thread.438753/page-71

Page 82: Laughing Japanese soldier was created by the editor using Nightcafé https://creator.nightcafe.studio/

Printed in the USA
CPSIA information can be obtained
at www.ICGtesting.com
CBHW060549250924
14863CB00053B/1010

9 781763 669505